IMPERIAL RUSSIA AFTER 1861

Peaceful Modernization or Revolution?

PROBLEMS IN EUROPEAN CIVILIZATION

UNDER THE EDITORIAL DIRECTION OF

Ralph W. Greenlaw and Dwight E. Lee†*

DECLINE AND FALL OF THE ROMAN EMPIRE — *Why Did It Collapse?* †

THE PIRENNE THESIS — *Analysis, Criticism, and Revision**

THE CORONATION OF CHARLEMAGNE — *What Did It Signify?* *

THE GREGORIAN EPOCH — *Reformation, Revolution, Reaction?* *

INNOCENT III — *Vicar of Christ or Lord of the World?* †

THE CRUSADES — *Motives and Achievements**

THE RENAISSANCE — *Medieval or Modern?* *

MACHIAVELLI — *Cynic, Patriot, or Political Scientist?* *

THE REFORMATION — *Material or Spiritual?* *

THE "NEW MONARCHIES" AND REPRESENTATIVE ASSEMBLIES — *Medieval Constitutionalism or Modern Absolutism?* *

THE CHARACTER OF PHILIP II — *The Problem of Moral Judgments in History**

THE THIRTY YEARS' WAR — *Problems of Motive, Extent, and Effect**

PROTESTANTISM AND CAPITALISM — *The Weber Thesis and Its Critics**

THE ORIGINS OF THE ENGLISH CIVIL WAR — *Conspiracy, Crusade, or Class Conflict?* *

THE REVOLUTION OF 1688 — *Whig Triumph or Palace Revolution?* †

PETER THE GREAT — *Reformer or Revolutionary?* †

THE GREATNESS OF LOUIS XIV — *Myth or Reality?* *

GEORGE III — *Tyrant or Constitutional Monarch?* *

THE EIGHTEENTH-CENTURY REVOLUTION — *French or Western?* †

THE INFLUENCE OF THE ENLIGHTENMENT ON THE FRENCH REVOLUTION — *Creative, Disastrous, or Non-Existent?* *

THE ECONOMIC ORIGINS OF THE FRENCH REVOLUTION — *Poverty or Prosperity?* *

METTERNICH, THE "COACHMAN OF EUROPE" — *Statesman or Evil Genius?* *

THE INDUSTRIAL REVOLUTION IN BRITAIN — *Triumph or Disaster?* *

ROMANTICISM — *Definition, Explanation, and Evaluation*†

1848 — *A Turning Point?* *

NAPOLEON III — *Buffoon, Modern Dictator, or Sphinx?* †

OTTO VON BISMARCK — *A Historical Assessment**

IMPERIAL RUSSIA AFTER 1861 — *Peaceful Modernization or Revolution?* †

THE "NEW IMPERIALISM" — *Analysis of Late Nineteenth-Century Expansion**

THE ANGLO-BOER WAR — *Why Was It Fought? Who Was Responsible?* †

A FREE CHURCH IN A FREE STATE? — *The Catholic Church, Italy, Germany, France, 1864–1914* †

THE DREYFUS AFFAIR — *A Tragedy of Errors?* †

THE OUTBREAK OF THE FIRST WORLD WAR — *Who Was Responsible?* *

THE RUSSIAN REVOLUTION AND BOLSHEVIK VICTORY — *Why and How?* *

THE VERSAILLES SETTLEMENT — *Was It Foredoomed to Failure?* *

THE STALIN REVOLUTION — *Fulfillment or Betrayal of Communism?* †

THE ETHIOPIAN CRISIS — *Touchstone of Appeasement?* *

THE NAZI REVOLUTION — *Germany's Guilt or Germany's Fate?* *

THE BRITISH IN INDIA — *Imperialism or Trusteeship?* †

THE OUTBREAK OF THE SECOND WORLD WAR — *Design or Blunder?* †

THE COLD WAR — *Ideological Conflict or Power Struggle?* †

Other volumes in preparation

IMPERIAL RUSSIA AFTER 1861

Peaceful Modernization or Revolution?

EDITED WITH AN INTRODUCTION BY

Arthur E. Adams

MICHIGAN STATE UNIVERSITY

D. C. HEATH AND COMPANY • BOSTON

Englewood • Chicago • Dallas • San Francisco • Atlanta • London • Toronto

Library of Congress Catalog Card Number 65–12695

PRINTED IN THE UNITED STATES OF AMERICA

Table of Contents

Part I

Introduction

I

TSAR Alexander II's emancipation of the serf in 1861 may legitimately serve as the starting point for an investigation of Russia's march toward its twentieth century revolutions. While the processes that eventually exploded into revolution began long before 1861, the emancipation signaled the beginning of a new phase in Russia's struggle for reform. Of necessity this decisive legislative action was followed by a number of others, which, taken together, exercised immense influence for change throughout the 56-year period between 1861 and 1917. All the reforms set in motion or accelerated intellectual, economic, political, and social developments which had somehow to be dealt with by the imperial government or by Russian society, since they threatened the existence of government and society alike.

The proximate causes of revolution in 1917 (as in 1905) were deep social and economic stresses, a disastrous war, an obdurate, apolitical Tsar, and political leaders who were fanatically determined to make revolution. In the longer view, the revolutions occurred because Russia failed to adjust rapidly and completely enough to the pressures for change that piled up after 1861.

The student who wishes to understand the course of Russia's history after the emancipation of the serf must seek answers for a number of fundamental questions: What were the problems and forces that drove Russia toward change? What role did each of these problems and forces play in the nation's headlong rush into the twentieth century? What action was needed to solve Russia's most difficult problems? And ultimately: Could Russia have completed the modernization of its political, social, and economic institutions peacefully, or was violent revolution both necessary and inevitable?

The answers to these questions have been and are subjects of controversy. Very few of the many interpretations set forth by those who have studied Russian affairs are accepted by all contending parties. Despite this lack of agreement, probably the best way for the student to gain a comprehension of this significant historical era is to read the answers proffered by the ablest minds that have pondered and written on Russia's difficulties. Such study will deepen his knowledge of the issues, personalities and historical processes involved; concurrently it will give him an understanding of the conflicting interpretive viewpoints (and the areas of consensus among them) that is essential if he is to make intelligent judgments for himself.

It is the purpose of this book to help the student to examine the conflict of opinion about Russia's destiny after 1861. This is accomplished by presenting a selective sample of the most significant analyses that have been made, both by men who lived and worked in Russia during the period covered and by later scholars.

These selections are divided into two parts. The purpose of Part I is to present the conflicting views of important Russian groups and their spokesmen (people contemporary to the era 1861–1917) about the nature of Russia's problems and the best means of solving them. In other words, for each of the reading selections in Part I the central issue is how one of these groups or its spokesmen answered the twofold question: *What is wrong with Russia, and what must be done to set things right?*

The views of four representative groups of people who were directly involved in Russia's struggle are considered. They are: the two wings of the radical intelligentsia —the *Populists* (Narodniki) and the *Marxists;* the *Liberals* (both of the gentry and the intelligentsia); and the *Official-Conservatives* (defined here as the Tsars and their principal ministers). This is not an exhaustive presentation of every important body of opinion in Russia; nor do the selections included present all the numerous shadings of opinion that existed within the four selected groups; for example, a broader definition of the conservative group would embrace not only the Official-Conservatives included in these readings, but important scholars, authors and public figures outside government circles who were most critical of official policies. Nevertheless, it is safe to say that the four groups listed above represent Russia's most significant and influential trends of thought after 1861.

The selections in Part II present the views of twentieth-century scholars. Even the most brilliant and detached of Russia's radicals, liberals and conservatives were necessarily denied the later scholar's perspective and historical objectivity. Since the aim of this work is to explore as fully as space permits the entire spectrum of opinion about Russia's situation and expectations after 1861, it is essential to examine the views of recent scholars who have set down their interpretations after exhaustive and dispassionate examination of the evidence. These men, too, attempt to answer the twofold question to which the groups of Part I addressed themselves, but for the scholars the tense is necessarily changed: *What were Russia's problems, and what was needed to correct them?* As the reader will observe, each individual scholar's views conflict with those of the representative groups and, to a lesser degree, with one another. Presentation of these views rounds out the examination of the conflict of opinion and provides the student with additional evidence about the era under study.

II

In order to facilitate a clear understanding of the opinions expressed in these readings, it should be said that each of the representative groups contemporary to 1861–1917 tended in general to identify four primary problems.[1] Thus, when analyzing the Russian situation, they habitually identified the central problems as *ideological, agrarian, industrial,* and *political.* When they discussed what had to be done to save Russia, the action they advocated also fell into these four categories. Naturally the four primary problems are not equally stressed in every reading, mainly because the groups differed in their evaluation of the significance of the separate problems. For example, to the Populists, the agrarian situation and its improvement were of prime importance, whereas the Marxists emphasized the significance of the growth of capitalism and the role of the urban proletariat. Another variation of coverage appears when the views of a single spokesman are presented. Thus, in Section 3 of Part I, the first official-conservative representative, Konstantin Pobedonostsev, addresses himself almost wholly to ideological and political problems simply because he had little interest in and almost no knowledge of economic affairs. In the selection following, the Tsar's Minister of Finance, Sergei Witte, focuses wholly upon the necessity to carry through Russia's industrialization, a viewpoint clearly determined by his professional interests.

Because the student needs to recognize at once the primary problems being discussed at any moment in each of the selec-

[1] A primary problem may be defined for the purpose of the present study as one causing such serious economic, political or social stresses that its immediate solution was felt to be imperative.

tions, these problems are defined more fully below:

(1) *The Ideological Problem.* After 1861, as before, the question that most concerned Russia's educated people was: What should be the fundamental intellectual and moral foundations of Russian society? Stated in their more extreme form the two answers most commonly given were, on the one side, *the rationalist and humanist ideas of the West,* and opposed to these, *Russian Tsardom's traditionalist, authoritarian and Orthodox Christian ideas.* There was no escaping the conflicts which this dichotomy of views created. It should be noted in passing, however, that the debate after 1861 was only a sharp and crucial phase of an older struggle. Since the sixteenth century, Western ideas and Western institutions had presented Muscovy with a painful dilemma that may be stated in a somewhat oversimplified way thus: Should Russia adopt the West's political, economic, and social ideas and institutions, along with its science, technology, literature, and art, at the risk of sacrificing "true Russian" ideas and institutions, including in all probability the autocracy and the authority of the faith? Or: Should Russia preserve its old ways of thinking and acting and fend off the most "dangerous" Western influences? After the Crimean War (1853–1856) the choice was made all the more difficult by the suspicion that any attempt to preserve old Russia would spell the nation's eclipse as a Great Power.

In the first years of the eighteenth century, Peter the Great struggled vigorously to westernize Russia, repudiating most of its inheritance.[2] Later in that century, his distinguished successor, Catherine, while playing like a fascinated moth around the dazzling lights of Western thought, clung steadfastly to the Russian principles buttressing her authority. During the first sixty years of the nineteenth century, many nobles and newly-educated members of the lower classes embraced Western ideas with passionate abandon and dedicated their lives to bringing Russian life into harmony with Western models, but Slavophil thinkers and many officials grimly opposed such westernizing. Shocked by the disparity between their Western ideals and the grim circumstances of Russian life, which they blamed upon the traditionalism of the political regime, radicals and liberals sought to reform their motherland. This was to be their aim through the rest of the century. They attacked the principles of autocracy, the Orthodox faith and what seemed to them to be the stagnation and sterility of Russian culture, and they disseminated widely their Western ideas and plans for reform. When they attempted to implement their beliefs, some went directly to the workers and peasants, hoping by education and assistance to rouse these classes from their lethargy; others placed their faith in economic development, achieved by one or another method. Some sought to compel governmental reform by attacking officials with bombs and guns, or advocated total destruction of the *ancien régime.* Later, when newly-formed political parties placed representatives in the dumas of the early twentieth century, members of the liberal intelligentsia sought to introduce reform by legal and constitutional means. And always the Tsar and most of his leading officials, though sensitive to ideas from the West and aware that adjustment to these ideas was necessary, if only for the sake of improved efficiency and greater national power, resolutely defended the traditions and institutions of the Russian autocracy.

All educated men after 1861 knew that it was imperative to decide which intellectual and moral principles would predominate in Russia and determine the course of her development. But there were many views and no simple way of selecting the best of them. Thus, while discussion and debate ran on almost without end, much-needed decisions were often prevented, or the process of selection was un-

[2] See Marc Raeff, ed. *Peter the Great, Problems in European Civilization,* Boston, 1963.

duly influenced, now by one dominant force, now by another.

(2) *The Agrarian Problem.* Emancipation did not solve the agrarian problem. In the settlements that followed 1861, the "freed" serf, dealing at a disadvantage with his former lord, did not receive the land he had expected. Frequently his portion was less than he had tilled prior to the reform; in general he was overcharged for what he did receive. For his small plot he owed redemption payments and taxes often exceeding his income. Personally, the peasant was pinned to the land, literally enslaved to the commune (*mir*), which was made responsible for collecting his redemption obligations and which actually controlled the land he was supposed to own. Although the agrarian areas were increasingly embarrassed by a rapid population growth, the communes grimly held on to their surplus manpower. Meanwhile, peasant methods of cultivation continued to produce low crop yields. All this directly aggravated the peasants' impoverishment. Russia, it was clear, would remain poor and profoundly dissatisfied unless the agrarian problem was solved effectively; yet, such was the urgent need of economic development in other fields that the peasant was virtually sacrificed for the sake of industrialization.

For the agrarian problem, the question "What is to be done?" was critical, but the answers of radicals, liberals and conservatives were diverse, and the government made no major effort to implement a workable solution until after the revolution of 1905. Then, the astute Minister of the Interior, P. A. Stolypin, made it possible for industrious peasants to leave the mir and to hold their land as individual owners. Concurrently, in the years after 1905, redemption payments were ended, the government provided increased facilities for technical assistance and credit, and peasant resettlement of the Siberian lands was encouraged. Stolypin's reforms aroused great hope, for they appeared to offer Russia a way out of the agrarian tangle, but before this alternative could be fully exploited, the First World War intervened.

(3) *The Problem of Industrialization.* Backward economically, unable to compete successfully with Western military forces, slipping from its position as a Great Power, Russia faced the problem of industrial development, and at least some of its leaders understood that it must catch up with the Western Powers or fail in the race for national prestige and prosperity. But this problem involved much more than the empire's need for economic and military strength; it was also a matter of great social concern. Russia's economic poverty and low productivity, its need to buy manufactured goods from abroad at high prices with money gained by exporting agricultural produce or borrowed from foreign banks, spelled suffering without adequate improvement. The important question was: How can economic development be achieved rapidly enough to satisfy Russia's needs, with a minimum of unnecessary personal sacrifice and a maximum of social justice?

In the 90's the government made swift industrialization the center of its program for economic development. The policy of force-feeding big iron, steel, and machine industries by rapid expansion of railways placed heavy demands upon the peasant in the form of excessive taxes; thus it hindered the development of an internal market other than the state itself. Seeking to raise Russia by her boot-straps, the state offered the land as a sort of colony for foreign exploitation. It was hoped that foreign capital would create industries, which in turn would create their own capital. As will be seen (Part I, Section 3), Russia's most distinguished Minister of Finance, Sergei Witte, literally begged his Tsar to support a firm policy that would get the country through this painful transition period as quickly as possible.

Objections to the government's policies were numerous and forceful. The Russo-Japanese War of 1905, followed by the First World War, tragically underlined the still unfinished character of industrial development. Nevertheless, in spite of stresses and maladjustments resulting from this policy, Russia by 1914 was well along the road to industrialization.

(4) *The Problem of Political Reform.* Even the Tsars' ministers recognized the need for political reform, but this term was variously defined by contending parties. To the terrorist it meant an end to imperial rule, even if this required assassination of the reigning Tsar; to the liberal gentry it meant cautious evolution; to the liberal intelligentsia of 1905 it meant limitation of royal authority and establishment of a constitutional monarchy. To Lenin's Marxists it meant erecting a dictatorship of the proletariat controlled by its so-called "vanguard," the Bolshevik Party; and to the Tsars' highest officials it meant creating a stronger, more efficient government, capable of enforcing economic plans, carrying out reforms at its own speed, and suppressing criticism.

It should be noted that there were serious disagreements *within* each major group. Among the many factions of the radical intelligentsia violent argument raged about such matters as the kinds of reform needed, the degree of change to be demanded, and the timing of revolution. Inside the liberal camp there were two clearly-defined streams of thought. And in the government, more than one minister who formulated wise and progressive policies found them blocked by a stubborn Tsar or some devious court intrigue. The result of such unresolved divergences of opinion was an endless chain of conflict that neutralized many good intentions, crippled intelligent reform efforts, and thus contributed to the development of ever more extreme and ungovernable pressures for change.

III

A number of what may be termed *active forces* significantly influenced the course of events in Russia after 1861. In some cases these were individual men or aggregates of men (as, for example, the representative Russian groups already identified). Intellectual and political zealots fought to introduce change, or energetically opposed it; less politically conscious elements (such as the peasantry) pressed almost blindly for relief from deprivation and injustice. In addition there were impersonal but dynamic historical forces at work: the growing need for governmental reform and economic development, the expanding acceptance of new political ideas. Incessantly interacting upon one another, these forces helped to form the moving matrix in which modern Russia developed.

It is obvious that an awareness of the active forces and their impact upon Russian affairs is essential to the student. The following paragraphs divide the most important of them into three broad categories and briefly describe their roles.

(1) *The Actions of the Intellectuals.* The perceptive student will realize at once that the representative groups whose views he is studying—the radicals, the liberals, and the official-conservatives—were not mere observers passively viewing Russia's agony. On the contrary, these groups and their members played vigorous roles as human actors in Russia's great drama, and they were very influential in helping to determine Russia's fate. These human actors expressed concretely the conflict of opinion in deed as well as in thought. Not only did they study and write about Russia's problems; by their actions they also solved some of these problems or made their solution virtually impossible. The most spectacular evidence of the radical intelligentsia's influence is provided by the terrorist acts of its more violent members; for example, the assassinations of Alexander II, Stolypin, and several thousand lesser officials and private citizens. Although the liberals' actions were less dramatic, one should not underestimate the eventually successful pressures of the liberal intelligentsia for constitutional reform. And above all it should be remembered that the views of the official-conservatives, strongly supported by influential elements

of Russian society, were regularly translated into government policy. These officials implemented the reforms of 1861 and after; they deliberately accelerated the processes of industrialization, found ways to ameliorate the agrarian situation, and so on; in short, as the governors of Russia they played a decisive role in Russia's modernization.

All these groups desperately tried to cope with the changing conditions of Russian life. Each had constantly to adapt to new situations, to analyze the dynamic developments of Russia and to devise new means of solving the primary problems. Within an agitated milieu in which the actors were swept along by rapidly moving events, every faction groped for some means of influencing affairs, whether its hope was to rein in what more and more resembled a runaway society or to hurry it on its road to destruction. It is small wonder that there was confusion and waste, quarreling and debate about the meaning of events; small wonder, too, that the primary problems were not finally solved when so many conflicting factions sought to force their solutions upon one another.

Information about the conflict of deeds parallels the conflict of opinion in several of the following selections. As he reads, the student may well ponder on the irony of a situation in which well-intentioned men holding diverse opinions, acted, sometimes inadvertently, to make the peaceful solution of Russia's problems exceedingly difficult.

(2) *The Influence of Workers and Peasants.* In contrast to the active roles of the intellectuals, two other groups (not represented directly in the selections presented below, but discussed on many pages) exercised a vastly different sort of influence upon events. These were the relatively small group of urbanized industrial workers and the great mass of the peasantry. The first gained importance late in the nineteenth century and became an effective instrument for political action under the promptings of the radical intelligentsia early in the twentieth century. The peasantry—unorganized, angry, widely dispersed, illiterate, and poorly led—was politically ineffective, except when its local jacqueries became so numerous as to be almost universal. Yet the peasants' dissatisfactions made them a great reservoir of frustration and unrest that influenced all the intellectual groups and helped to undermine the imperial system.

(3) *The Dynamic Historical Process.* Russia's modernization was ruthlessly pushed by a series of historical processes whose consequences could not easily be avoided. These processes seemed to evolve according to some inner logic or system of dynamics of their own, disregarding the human beings who attempted to control them, or even subjecting those human beings to their developmental laws. The rule of these processes was change, often so swift and all-embracing that to comprehend and regulate it overtaxed the ability of the leaders of Russian thought and government.

In retrospect the general course of some of these processes can be so closely charted that one may watch event follow event in what appears to be a rigid progression of cause and effect. Consider, for example, the consequences of the emancipation in Russia as examined by Lazar Volin in Part II. Given the botched, unsatisfactory character of the emancipation legislation and its implementation, it seems to us almost inevitable that the peasant became increasingly restless and land-hungry, that his situation prolonged his inefficiency and ignorance and intensified his dissatisfaction with the regime, that in time young workers found ways to escape from the communes into the cities, and that half-hearted, piecemeal reforms only worsened the general situation. Similarly, as the selection in Part II by Alexander Gershenkron illustrates, once serious efforts were begun to industrialize the country, it is as though the dynamics of industrialization took over and began to dictate their requirements to Russia's rulers and people. Industrialization demands capital, labor forces, raw materials, markets, trained technicians, and managers; and nations that seek to industrialize must provide these necessities or lose their initial investments as well as their hope for modernization. In the case of Russia, the effort to make such provision had unfortunate but seemingly unavoidable side effects; for, as has been noted, it compelled agents of government to exploit the peasant in favor of industry.

Consider still another example of the dynamic social process in action. In the area of intellectual affairs one can clearly see a system of ideas like that of Marxism drop into the turgid sea of Russian thought and steadily widen the ripples of its influence until even Marxism's fiercest enemies were forced to think within the framework of its concepts and to employ its terms in their writings.

The relationships between these dynamic historical processes and the men who sought to direct or control them in the years after 1861 are almost infinitely complex. Yet whoever seeks to understand the march toward revolution must be sensitively aware of the interplay between these impersonal and sometimes imponderable forces and Russia's institutions and men.

IV

Much of the evidence presented in these selections argues that, at least until the First World War, revolution was neither inevitable nor necessary, although some of the representative groups insisted that it was both, and individual leaders acted in such a way as to make it so. In particular, it is assumed by the scholars of Part II that revolution might have been avoided, if only one or another of the important men or groups had acted differently.

Undoubtedly the historical figures whose ideas and deeds are considered in these selections must be assigned a high degree of responsibility for the coming of revolution, although this is not to say categorically that these men could have prevented revolution. Certainly one of Russia's deepest tragedies lies in the fact that after moving mountains with the great reforms, with industrialization and promising political innovations, the nation's governing officials and active social elements failed or refused to come to terms with one another. While it is true that great historical forces can be too powerful to be easily diverted or resisted, the human actors of history invariably enjoy some freedom of choice. And, unquestionably, many of the important leaders of Russian affairs could have made wiser and more responsible decisions than they did — on a host of issues. Yet these considerations are not sufficient to justify laying the responsibility for revolution wholly upon the human actors. One cannot blame a Stolypin for being what he was, a brilliant and loyal representative of the service nobility; nor is it reasonable to conclude that the Cadet party should have followed a policy of conciliation toward the government, knowing that it would lose its popular support by so doing. Russia's problems were chaotically complicated; the time and means for making effective adjustment to the pressures for change were limited; the institutional and traditional barriers to change were high and strong.

Thus, the tantalizing question remains open: Could Russia's leaders have avoided revolution? It is difficult not to cast one's mind back along the corridors of Russia's history after 1861, searching for those important moments when an act of statesmanship or a few lines read into the scene differently by a Witte, a Lenin, a Miliukov, or one of the Tsars, might have moved Russia away from the holocaust of revolution. Soviet scholars, of course, continue to argue in the Marxist-Leninist tradition that revolution was inevitable. While the question cannot be settled finally, recent Western scholars are inclined to insist that at least until 1914–1917 there were grounds for believing that Russia could work out her road to modernization peacefully, that in fact, in an improving economic milieu, government officials and duma leaders were gaining the experience and maturity needed to transform the parliamentary experiment into an effective political system. But when war came, it appears, the die was cast. Too many unsolved problems had been allowed to pile up, and neither the government nor the old social order had the strength to ride through new and great crises.

In the present era, the question of whether or not the revolution could have been avoided is far from being academic. To those who count costs in terms of human suffering, the most bitter thought of all is that the Russian people probably could have bettered their present achievements in economic and social justice and political freedom had they not squandered so much of their substance upon an extravagantly costly revolution. Viewed in today's international context, this probability has very real significance and applicability, particularly for the underdeveloped nations of Latin America, Africa, and Asia that are seeking to modernize themselves as Russia so desperately struggled to do before 1917. Russia's tragic experience underlines how imperative it is that wisdom and statesmanship predominate over violence during the delicate and complex process of modernization. The leaders of the developing nations, as well as the people of Western countries endeavoring to help them, would do well to re-examine Russia's historical development after 1861, if only to learn how some of the most costly errors the Russians made may be avoided today and tomorrow.

[NOTE: Almost all footnote references have been omitted from the selections that follow.]

The Conflict of Opinion

Part I

The Radical Intelligentsia

"[The Populists] . . . looked on government and the social structure of their country as a moral and political monstrosity — obsolete, barbarous, stupid, and odious — and dedicated their lives to its total destruction."

— Isaiah Berlin

"When Lenin called himself a Marxist it meant, to him, that he had accepted the axiom of the moral and actual inevitability of the proletarian revolution. . . . This revolution was seen as . . . the seizure of power by the leaders of the proletariat, so that the establishment of a proletarian dictatorship was Lenin's guiding aim."

— Alfred G. Meyer

The Liberals

". . . in Russia, a have-not liberalism as a rule oscillated between the prosaic compromises of 'small deeds' and the opposite extreme of 'senseless dreams.' "

— George Fischer

The Official-Conservatives

"The whole secret of Russian order and prosperity is in the top, in the person of the supreme authority."

— Konstantin Pobedonostsev

"We have to develop mass-production industries, widely dispersed and variegated, in which not customs duties, but the more powerful and beneficial laws of competition play the dominant role."

— Sergei Witte

"Stolypin thus set forth his goal as a reformer and statesman: to create a strong peasantry of individual landowners who would be the mainstay of the crown and the most formidable rampart against the spread of revolution."

— Leonid I. Strakhovsky

Part II

Progress in Modernization

"It seems legitimate to speculate that if a prolonged and exhausting war, culminating in a revolution and civil war, had not intervened in 1914–1918, agricultural improvement would have continued. If, in conjunction with such progress, the Stolypin policy of the 'wager on the strong' could have been further implemented for a period of several decades, it is possible, though by no means certain, that the projected bulwark against an agrarian revolution might have been created."

— LAZAR VOLIN

"The industrialization between 1906 and 1914 no longer offers a picture of a race against time and of progressive exhaustion, physically and mentally, of the population's power to suffer and endure. . . . One might surmise that in the absence of the war Russia could have continued on the road of progressive westernization."

— ALEXANDER GERSHENKRON

Unsolved Problems

"The vital struggle in the last decades of the empire was that which was going on within the government between those who supported the traditional autocracy to the bitter end, and those who favored the transformation of Russia into a modern bureaucratic and constitutional state. . . . The fragmentation of Russian politics at this stage was such that the collapse of the autocracy in 1917 resulted in a situation in which no alternative had any wide support."

— CYRIL E. BLACK

"Industrialism was beyond . . . [Nicholas II's] understanding, revolutionaries were to him simply manifestations of evil to be crushed at any cost, good government not an ideal to be sought but an irrelevance compared to the fulfilment of the commands of his ancestors and the maintenance of the loyalty of the Russian people to his own person. . . ."

— DONALD W. TREADGOLD

THE RADICAL INTELLIGENTSIA (POPULISTS AND MARXISTS)

The Populists' Moral Condemnation of Russia's Political and Social Systems

SIR ISAIAH BERLIN

Except for the war years when he served in the British embassies at Washington and Moscow, much of Isaiah Berlin's working life has been spent at Oxford. Educated at Corpus Christi College, he began his career as lecturer in philosophy at New College over thirty years ago and, since 1957, has been Chichele Professor of Social and Political Theory in All Souls' College. His philosophically inclined historical studies include *Karl Marx* (1939), *The Inevitability of History* (1954), *The Age of Enlightenment* (1956), and *Moses Hess* (1958). In the selection presented below, he carefully analyzes the complex ideas and motivations of the Russian Populists. Lighted by vast knowledge and a profound sympathy for the men described, Professor Berlin's analysis is remarkable for its humanity, accuracy, and comprehensiveness.

RUSSIAN Populism is the name not of a single political party, nor of a coherent body of doctrine, but of a widespread radical movement in Russia in the middle of the nineteenth century. It was born during the great social and intellectual ferment which followed the death of Tsar Nicholas I and the defeat and humiliation of the Crimean War, grew to fame and influence during the 'sixties and 'seventies, and reached its culmination with the assassination of Tsar Alexander II, after which it swiftly declined. Its leaders were men of very dissimilar origins, outlooks and capacities; it was not at any stage more than a loose congeries of small independent groups of conspirators or their sympathizers, who sometimes united for common action, and at other times operated in isolation. These groups tended to differ both about ends and about means. Nevertheless they held certain fundamental beliefs in common, and possessed sufficient moral and political solidarity to entitle them to be called a single movement. Like their predecessors, the Decembrist conspirators in the 'twenties, and the circles that gathered round Herzen and Belinsky in the 'thirties and 'forties, they looked on the government and the social structure of their country as a moral and political monstrosity — obsolete, barbarous, stupid and odious — and dedicated their lives to its total destruction. Their general ideas were not original. They shared the democratic ideals of the European radicals of their day, and in addition believed that the struggle between social and economic classes was the determining factor in politics; they held this theory not in its Marxist form (which did not effectively reach

Russia until the 'seventies) but in the form in which it was taught by Proudhon and Herzen, and before them by Saint-Simon, Fourier and other French socialists and radicals whose writings had entered Russia, legally and illegally, in a thin but steady stream, for several decades.

The theory of social history as dominated by the class war — the heart of which is the notion of the coercion of the "have-nots" by the "haves" — was born in the course of the Industrial Revolution in the West; and its most characteristic concepts belong to the capitalist phase of economic development. Economic classes, capitalism, cut-throat competition, proletarians and their exploiters, the evil power of unproductive finance, the inevitability of increasing centralization and standardization of all human activities, the transformation of men into commodities and the consequent "alienation" of individuals and groups and degradation of human lives—these notions are fully intelligible only in the context of expanding industrialism. Russia, even as late as the 'fifties, was one of the least industrialized states in Europe. Nevertheless, exploitation and misery had long been amongst the most familiar and universally recognized characteristics of its social life, the principal victims of the system being the peasants, both serfs and free, who formed over nine-tenths of its population. An industrial proletariat had indeed come into being, but by mid-century did not exceed 2 or 3 per cent of the population of the Empire. Hence the cause of the oppressed was still at that date overwhelmingly that of the agricultural workers who formed the lowest stratum of the population, the vast majority being serfs in state or private possession. The Populists looked upon them as martyrs whose grievances they were determined to avenge and remedy, and as embodiments of simple uncorrupted virtue, whose social organization (which they largely idealized) was the natural foundation on which the future of Russian society must be rebuilt. The central Populist goals were social justice and social equality. Most of them were convinced, following Herzen, whose revolutionary propaganda in the 'fifties influenced them more than any other single set of ideas, that the essence of a just and equal society existed already in the Russian peasant commune—the *obshchina,* organized in the form of a collective unit called the *mir*. The *mir* was a free association of peasants which periodically redistributed the agricultural land to be tilled; its decisions bound all its members, and constituted the corner-stone on which, so the Populists maintained, a federation of socialized, self-governing units, conceived along lines popularized by the French socialist Proudhon, could be erected. The Populist leaders believed that this form of cooperation offered the possibility of a free and democratic social system in Russia, originating as it did in the deepest moral instincts and traditional values of Russian, and indeed all human, society, and they believed that the workers (by which they meant all productive human beings), whether in town or country, could bring this system into being with a far smaller degree of violence or coercion than had occurred in the industrial West. This system, since it alone sprang naturally from fundamental human needs and a sense of the right and the good that existed in all men, would ensure justice, equality and the widest opportunity for the full development of human faculties. As a corollary of this, the Populists believed that the development of large-scale centralized industry was not "natural," and therefore led inexorably to the degradation and dehumanization of all those who were caught in its tentacles: capitalism was an appalling evil, destructive of body and soul; but it was not inescapable. They denied that social or economic progress was necessarily bound up with the Industrial Revolution. They maintained that the application of scientific truths and methods to social and individual problems (in which they passionately believed), although it might, and often did, lead to the growth of capitalism, could be realized without this fatal sacrifice. They believed that it was possible to improve life by scientific techniques without necessarily destroying the "natural" life of the peasant village, or creating a vast, pauperized, faceless city proletariat. Capitalism seemed irresistible only because it had not been sufficiently resisted. However it might be in the West, in Russia "the curse of bigness" could still be successfully fought, and federations of small self-governing units of producers, as Fourier and Proudhon had advocated, could be fostered, and indeed created, by deliberate action. Like their French masters, the Russian disciples held the institution of the state in particular hatred, since to them it was at once the symbol, the result, and the main source of injustice and inequality — a weapon wielded by the governing class to defend its own privileges — and one that, in the face of increasing resistance from its victims, grew progressively more brutal and blindly destructive. The defeat of liberal and radical movements in the West in 1848–9 confirmed them in their conviction that salvation did not lie in politics or political parties: it seemed clear to them that liberal parties and their leaders had neither understood nor made a serious effort to forward the fundamental interests of the oppressed populations of their countries. What the vast majority of peasants in Russia (or workers in Europe) needed was to be fed and clothed, to be given physical security, to be rescued from disease, ignorance, poverty and humiliating inequalities. As for political rights, votes, parliaments, republican forms, these were meaningless and useless to ignorant, barbarous, half-naked and starving men; such programmes merely mocked their misery. The Populists shared with the nationalistic Russian Slavophils (with whose political ideas they had otherwise little in common) a loathing of the rigidly class-conscious social pyramid of the West that was complacently accepted, or fervently believed in, by the conformist bourgeoisie and the bureaucracy to whom this bourgeoisie looked up.

The satirist Saltykov, in his famous dialogue between a German and a Russian boy, immortalized this attitude when he declared his faith in the Russian boy, hungry and in rags, stumbling in the mud and squalor of the accursed, slave-owning Tsarist régime, because he had not, like the neat, docile, smug, well-fed, well-dressed German boy, bartered away his soul for the sixpence that the Prussian official had offered him, and was consequently still capable, if only he was allowed to do so (as the German boy no longer was), of rising one day to his full human height. Russia was in darkness and in chains, but her spirit was not captive; her past was black, but her future promised more than the death in life of the civilized middle classes in Germany or France or England, who had long ago sold themselves for material security and had become so apathetic in their shameful, self-imposed servitude that they no longer knew how to want to be free.

The Populists, unlike the Slavophils, did not believe in the unique character or destiny of the Russian people. They were not mystical nationalists. They believed only that Russia was a backward nation which had not reached the stage of social and economic development at which the Western nations (whether or not they could have avoided this) had entered upon the path of unrestrained industrialism. They were not, for the most part, historical determinists; consequently they believed that it was possible for a nation in such a predicament to avoid this fate by the exercise of intelligence and will. They saw no reason why Russia could not benefit by Western science and Western technology without paying the appalling price paid by the West. They argued that it was possible to avoid the despotism of a centralized economy or a centralized government by adopting a loose, federal structure composed of self-governing, socialized units both of producers and of consumers. They held that it was desirable to organize, but not to lose sight of other values in the pursuit of organization as an end in itself; to be governed primarily by ethical and humanitarian and not solely by economic and technological — "ant-hill" — considerations. They declared that to protect human individuals against exploitation by turning them into an industrial army of collectivized robots was self-stultifying and suicidal. Ideas of the Populists were often unclear, and there were sharp differences among them, but there was an area of agreement wide enough to constitute a genuine movement. Thus they accepted, in broad outline, the educational and moral lessons, but not the state worship, of Rousseau. Some of them — indeed perhaps the majority — shared Rousseau's belief in the goodness of simple men, his conviction that the cause of corruption is the crippling effect of bad institutions, his acute distrust of all forms of cleverness, of intellectuals and specialists, of all self-isolating *côteries* and factions. They accepted the anti-political ideas, but not the technocratic centralism, of Saint-Simon. They shared the belief in conspiracy and violent action preached by Babeuf and his disciple Buonarroti, but not their Jacobin authoritarianism. They stood with Sismondi and Proudhon and Lamennais and the other originators of the notion of the welfare state, against, on the one hand, *laissez faire,* and, on the other, central authority, whether nationalist or socialist, whether temporary or permanent, whether preached by List, or Mazzini, or Lassalle, or Marx. They came close at times to the positions of Western Christian socialists, without, however, any religious faith, since like the French Encyclopaedists of the previous century, they believed in "natural" morality and scientific truth. These were some of the beliefs that held them together. But they were divided by differences no less profound.

The first and greatest of their problems was their attitude towards the peasants in whose name all that they did was done. Who was to show the peasants the true path to justice and equality? Individual liberty is not, indeed, condemned by the Populists, but it tends to be regarded as a liberal catchword, liable to distract attention from immediate social and economic tasks. Should one train experts to teach the ignorant younger brothers — the tillers of the soil, and, if need be, stimulate them to resist authority, to revolt and destroy the old order before the rebels had themselves fully grasped the need or meaning of such acts? That is the view of such dissimilar figures as Bakunin and Speshnev in the 'forties; it was preached by Chernyshevsky in the 'fifties, and was passionately advocated by Zaichnevsky and the Jacobins of "Young Russia" in the 'sixties; it was preached by Lavrov in the 'seventies and 'eighties, and equally by his rivals and opponents — the believers in disciplined professional terrorism — Nechaev and Tkachev, and their followers who include — for this purpose alone — not only the Socialist-Revolutionaries but also some of the most fanatical Russian Marxists, in particular Lenin and Trotsky.

Some among them asked whether this training of revolutionary groups might not create an arrogant *élite* of seekers of power and autocracy, men who would, at best, believe it their duty to give the peasants not what the peasants asked for but what they, their self-appointed mentors, thought good for them, namely, that which the masses ought to ask for, whether they in fact did so or not. They pushed the question further, and asked whether this would not, in due course, breed fanatical men who would pay too little heed to the actual wants of the vast majority of the Russian population, intent on forcing upon them only what they — the dedicated order of professional revolutionaries, cut off from the life of the masses by their own special training and conspiratorial lives — had chosen for them, ignoring the hopes and protests of the people itself. Was there not a terrible danger here of the substitution of a new yoke for the old, of a despotic oligarchy of intellectuals in the place of the nobility and the bureaucracy and the Tsar? What reason was there for thinking that the new masters would prove less oppressive than the old? This was argued by some among the terrorists of the 'sixties — Ishutin and Karakozov, for example — and even more forcibly by the majority of the idealistic young men, who "went among the people" in the 'seventies and later, with the aim not so much of teaching others as of themselves learning how to live, in a state of mind inspired by Rousseau (and perhaps by Nekrasov or Tolstoy) at least as much as by more tough-minded social theorists. These young men, the so called "repentant gentry," believed themselves to have been corrupted not merely by an evil social system but by the very process of liberal education which makes for deep inequalities and inevitably lifts scientists, writers, professors, experts, civilized men in general, too high above the heads of the masses, and so itself becomes the richest breeding-ground of injustice and class oppression; everything that obstructs understanding between individuals or groups or nations, that creates and keeps in being obstacles to human solidarity and fraternity, is *eo ipso* evil; specialization and university education build walls between men, prevent individuals and groups from "connecting," kill love and friendship, and are among the major causes responsible for what, after Hegel and his followers, came to be called the "alienation" of entire orders or classes or cultures. Some among the Populists contrived to ignore or evade this problem. Bakunin, for example, who, if he was not a Populist himself, influenced Populism profoundly, denounced faith in intellectuals and experts as liable to lead to the most ignoble of tyrannies — the rule of scientists and pedants — but would not face the problem of whether the revolutionaries had come to teach or to learn. It was left unanswered by the terrorists of the "People's Will" and their sympathizers. More sensitive and morally scrupulous thinkers — Chernyshevsky and Kropotkin, for example — felt the oppressive weight of the question, and did not attempt to conceal it from themselves; yet whenever they asked themselves by what right they proposed to impose this or that system of social organization on the mass of peasants who had grown up in a wholly different way of life, that might embody far profounder values of its own, they gave no clear reply. The question became even more acute when it was asked (as it increasingly came to be in the 'sixties) what was to be done if the peasants actually resisted the revolutionaries' plans for their liberation? Must the masses be deceived, or, worse still, coerced? No one denied that in the end it was the people, and not the revolutionary *élite,* that must govern, but in the meanwhile how far was one allowed to go in ignoring the majority's wishes, or in forcing them into courses which they plainly loathed? This was by no means a merely academic problem. The first enthusiastic adherents of radical Populism — the missionaries who went "to the people" in the famous summer of 1874 — were met by mounting indifference, suspicion, resentment and sometimes active hatred and resistance, on the part of their would-be beneficiaries who, as often as not, handed them over to the police. The Populists were thus forced to define their attitude explicitly, since they believed passionately in the need to justify their activities by rational argument. Their answers, when they came, were far from unanimous. The activists, men like Tkachev, Nechaev, and in a less political sense, Pisarev, whose admirers came to be known as Nihilists, anticipated Lenin in their contempt for democratic methods. Since the days of Plato, it had been argued that the spirit was superior to the flesh, and those who know must govern those who do not. The educated cannot listen to the uneducated and ignorant masses. The masses must be rescued by whatever means were available, if necessary against their own foolish wishes, by guile, or fraud, or violence if need be. But it was only a minority in the movement who accepted this division and the authoritarianism that it entailed: the majority were horrified by the open advocacy of such Machiavellian tactics, and thought that no end, however good, could fail to be destroyed by the adoption of monstrous means.

A similar conflict broke out over the attitude to the state. All Russian Populists were agreed that the state was the embodiment of a system of coercion and inequality, and therefore intrinsically evil; neither justice nor happiness was possible until it was eliminated. But in the meanwhile what was to be the immediate aim of the revolution? Tkachev is quite clear that until the capitalist enemy had been finally destroyed, the weapon of coercion — the pistol torn from his hand by the revolutionaries — must on no account be thrown away, but must itself be turned against him. In other words the machinery of the state must not be destroyed, but must be used against the inevitable counter-revolution; it cannot be dispensed with until the last enemy has been — in Proudhon's immortal phrase—successfully liquidated, and mankind consequently has no further need of any instrument of coercion. In this doctrine he was followed by Lenin more faithfully than mere adherence to the ambivalent Marxist formula about the dictatorship of the proletariat seemed to require. Lavrov, who represents the central stream of Populism, and reflects all its vacillations and confusions, characteristically advocated not indeed the immediate or total elimination of the state but its systematic reduction to something vaguely described as the "minimum." Chernyshevsky, who is the least anarchistic of the Populists, conceives of the state as the organizer and protector of the free associations of peasants or workers, and contrives to see it at once as centralized and decentralized, a guarantee of order and efficiency, and of equality and individual liberty too.

All these thinkers share one vast apocalyptic assumption: that once the reign of evil — autocracy, exploitation, inequality — is consumed in the fire of the revolution, there will arise naturally and spontaneously out of its ashes a natural, harmonious, just order, needing only the gentle guidance of the enlightened revolutionaries to attain to its proper perfection. This great Utopian dream, based on simple faith in regenerated human nature, was a vision which the Populists shared with Godwin and Bakunin, Marx and Lenin. Its heart is the pattern of sin and fall and resurrection — of the road to the earthly paradise the gates of which will only open if men find the one true way and follow it. Its roots lie deep in the religious imagination of mankind, and there is therefore nothing surprising in the fact that this secular version of it had strong affinities with the faith of the Russian Old Believers — the dissenting sects — for whom, since the great religious schism of the seventeenth century, the Russian state and its rulers, particularly Peter the Great, represented the rule of Satan upon earth; this persecuted religious underground provided a good many potential allies whom the Populists made efforts to mobilize. There were deep divisions among the Populists; they differed about the future rôle of the intellectuals, as compared with that of the peasants; they differed about the historical importance of the rising class of capitalists, gradualism versus conspiracy, education and propaganda versus terrorism and preparation for immediate risings. All these questions were interrelated and they demanded immediate solutions. But the deepest rift among the Populists arose over the urgent question of whether a truly democratic revolution could possibly occur before a sufficient number of the oppressed had become fully conscious — that is, capable of understanding and analysing the causes of their intolerable condition. The moderates argued that no revolution could justly be called democratic unless it sprang from the rule of the revolutionary majority. But in that event, there was perhaps no alternative to waiting until education and propaganda had created this majority — a course that was being advocated by almost all Western socialists — Marxist and non-Marxist alike — in the second half of the nineteenth century. Against this the Russian Jacobins argued that to wait, and in the meanwhile to condemn all forms of revolt organized by resolute minorities as irresponsible terrorism or, worse still, as the replacement of one despotism by another, would lead to catastrophic results: while the revolutionaries procrastinated, capitalism would develop rapidly; the breathing space would enable the ruling class to develop a social and economic base incomparably stronger than that which it possessed at present; the growth of a prosperous and energetic capitalism would create opportunities of employment for the radical intellectuals themselves: doctors, engineers, educators, economists, technicians, and experts of all types would be assigned profitable tasks and positions, nor would their new bourgeois masters (unlike the existing régime) seek to force them into any kind of political conformity; the intelligentsia would obtain special privileges, status and wide opportunities for self-expression — harmless radicalism would be tolerated, a good deal of personal liberty permitted — and in this way the revolutionary cause would lose its most valuable recruits. Once those whom insecurity and discontent had driven into making common cause with the oppressed had been partially satisfied, the incentive to revolutionary activity would be weakened, and the prospects of a radical transformation of society would become exceedingly dim. The radical wing of the revolutionaries argued with great force that the advance of capitalism, whatever Marx might say, was not inevitable; it might be so in Western Europe, but in Russia it could still be arrested by a revolutionary *coup,* destroyed in the root before it had had time to grow too strong. If recognition of the need to awaken the "political consciousness" of the majority of the workers and peasants (which by this time, and partly as a result of the failure of the intellectuals in 1848, had been pronounced absolutely indispensable to the revolution both by Marxists and by the majority of the Populist leaders) was tantamount to the adoption of a gradualist programme, the moment for action would surely be missed; in place of the Populist or socialist revolution would there not arise a vigorous, imaginative, predatory, successful capitalist régime which would succeed Russian semi-feudalism as surely as it had replaced the feudal order in Western Europe? And then who could tell how many decades or centuries might elapse before the arrival, at long last, of the revolution? And when it did arrive, who could tell what kind of order it would, by that time, install — resting upon what social basis?

All Populists were agreed that the village commune was the ideal embryo of those socialist groups on which the future society was to be based. But would the development of capitalism not automatically destroy the commune? And if it was maintained (although perhaps this was not explicitly asserted before the 'eighties) that capitalism was already destroying the *mir,* that the class struggle, as analysed by Marx, was dividing the villages as surely as the cities, then the plan of action was clear: rather than sit with folded hands and watch this disintegration fatalistically, resolute men could and must arrest this process, and save the village commune. Socialism, so the Jacobins argued, could be introduced by the capture of power to which all the energies of the revolutionaries must be bent, even at the price of postponing the task of educating the peasants in moral, social and political realities; indeed, such education could surely be promoted more rapidly and efficiently after the revolution had broken the resistance of the old régime. This line of thought, which bears an extraordinary resemblance, if not to the actual words, then to the policies pursued by Lenin in 1917, was basically very different from the older Marxist determinism. Its perpetual refrain was that there was no time to lose. Kulaks were devouring the poorer peasants in the country, capitalists were breeding fast in the towns. If the government possessed even a spark of intelligence, it would make concessions and promote reforms, and by this means divert educated men whose will and brain were needed for the revolution into the peaceful paths of the service of the reactionary state; propped up by such liberal measures, the unjust order would continue and be strengthened. The activists argued that there was nothing inevitable about revolutions: they were the fruit of human will and human reason. If there were not enough of these, the revolution might never take place at all. It was only the insecure who craved social solidarity and communal life; individualism was always a luxury, the ideal of the socially established. The new class of technical specialists — the modern, enlightened, energetic men celebrated by liberals like Kavelin and Turgenev, and at times, even by the radical individualist Pisarev — were for the Jacobin Tkachev "worse than cholera or typhus," for by applying scientific methods to social life they were playing into the hands of the new, rising capitalist oligarchs and thereby obstructing the path to freedom. Palliatives were fatal when only an operation could save the patient: it merely prolonged his disease and weakened him so much that in the end not even an operation could save him. One must strike before these new, potentially conformist, intellectuals had grown too numerous and too comfortable and had obtained too much power, for otherwise it would be too late: a Saint-Simonian *élite* of highly paid managers would preside over a new feudal order — an economically efficient but socially immoral society, inasmuch as it was based on permanent inequality.

The greatest of all evils was inequality. Whenever any other ideal came into conflict with equality, the Russian Jacobins always called for its sacrifice or modification; the first principle upon which all justice rested was that of equality; no society was equitable in which there was not a maximum degree of equality between men. If the revolution was to succeed, three major fallacies had to be fought and rooted out. The first was that men of culture alone created progress. This was not true, and had the bad consequence of inducing faith in *élites*. The second was the opposite illusion — that everything must be learnt from the common people. This was equally false. Rousseau's Arcadian peasants were so many idyllic figments. The masses were ignorant, brutal, reactionary and did not understand their own needs or good. If the revolution depended upon their maturity, or capacity for political judgment or organization, it would certainly fail. The last fallacy was that only a proletarian majority could successfully make a revolution. No doubt a proletarian majority might do that, but if Russia was to wait until it possessed one, the opportunity of destroying a corrupt and detested government would pass, and capitalism would be found to be too firmly in the saddle. What then must be done? Men must be trained to make the revolution and destroy the present system and all obstacles to social equality and democratic self-government. When this was achieved, a democratic assembly was to be convened, and if those who made the revolution took care to explain the reasons for it, and the social and economic situation that made it necessary, then the masses, benighted though they might be today, would assuredly, in the view of the Jacobins, grasp their condition sufficiently to allow themselves to be — indeed to welcome the opportunity of being — organized into the new free federation of productive associations. But supposing they were still, on the morrow of a successful *coup d'état,* not mature enough to see this? Herzen did indeed ask this awkward question again and again in his writings in the late 'sixties. The majority of the Populists were deeply troubled by it. But the activist wing had no doubt of the answer: strike the chains from the captive hero, and he will stretch himself to his full height and live in freedom and happiness for ever after. The views of these men were astonishingly simple. They believed in terrorism and more terrorism to achieve complete, anarchist, liberty. The purpose of the revolution, for them, was to establish absolute equality, not only economic and social, but "physical and physiological": they saw no discrepancy between this bed of Procrustes and absolute individual freedom. This order would be imposed in the beginning by the power and authority of the state, after which, the state, having fulfilled its purpose, would swiftly "liquidate" itself. Against this, the spokesmen of the main body of the Populists argued that Jacobin means tended to bring about Jacobin consequences: if the purpose of the revolution was to liberate, it must not use the weapons of despotism that were bound to enslave those whom they were designed to liberate: the remedy must not prove more destructive than the disease. To use the state to break the power of the exploiters and to impose a specific form of life upon a people, the majority of whom had not been educated to understand the need for it, was to exchange the Tsarist yoke for a new, not necessarily less crushing one — that of the revolutionary minority. The majority of the Populists were deeply democratic; they believed that all power tended to corrupt, that all concentration of authority tended to perpetuate itself, that all centralization was coercive and evil, and, therefore, that the sole hope of a just and free society lay in the peaceful conversion of men by rational argument to the truths of social and economic justice and democratic freedom. In order to obtain the opportunity of converting men to this vision, it might indeed be necessary to break the existing obstacles to free and rational intercourse — the police state, the power of capitalists or of landowners — and to use force in the process, whether mass mutiny or individual terrorism. But this concept of temporary measures presented itself to them as something wholly different from leaving absolute power in the hands of any party or group, however virtuous, once the power of the enemy had been broken. Their case is the classical case, during the last two centuries, of every libertarian and federalist against Jacobins and centralizers: it is Voltaire's case against both Helvétius and Rousseau; that of the left wing of the Gironde against the Mountain; Herzen used these arguments against the doctrinaire communists of the immediately preceding period — Cabet and the disciples of Babeuf; Bakunin denounced the Marxist demand for the dictatorship of the proletariat as something that would merely transfer power from one set of oppressors to another; the Populists of the 'eighties and 'nineties urged this against all those whom they suspected of conspiring (whether they realized this or not) to destroy individual spontaneity and freedom, whether they were *laissez faire* liberals who allowed factory owners to enslave the masses, or radical collectivists who were ready to do so themselves; whether they were promoters of capitalist combines or Marxist advocates of centralized authority; indeed they looked upon the entrepreneurs (as Mikhailovsky wrote to Dostoevsky in his celebrated criticism of his novel *The Possessed*) as the more dangerous — as brutal, amoral "social Darwinists," profoundly hostile to variety and individual freedom and character. This, again, was the main political issue which, at the turn of the century, divided the Russion Socialist-Revolutionaries from the Social-Democrats; and over which, a few years later, both Plekhanov and Martov broke with Lenin: indeed the great quarrel between the Bolsheviks and the Mensheviks (whatever its ostensible cause) turned upon it. In due course Lenin himself, two or three years after the October revolution, while he never abandoned the central Marxist doctrine, expressed his bitter disappointment with those very consequences of it which his opponents had predicted — bureaucracy and the arbitrary despotism of the party officials; and Trotsky accused Stalin of this same crime. The dilemma of means and ends is the deepest and most agonizing problem that torments the revolutionary movements of our own day in all the continents of the world, not least in Asia and Africa. That this debate took so clear and articulate a form within the Populist movement makes its development exceptionally relevant to our own predicament.

All these differences occurred within the framework of a common revolutionary outlook, for, whatever their disagreements, all Populists were united by an unshakable faith in the revolution. This faith derived from many sources. It sprang from the needs and outlook of a society still overwhelmingly pre-industrial, which gave the craving for simplicity and fraternity, and the agrarian idealism which derives ultimately from Rousseau — a reality which can still be seen in India and Africa today, and which necessarily looks Utopian to the eyes of social historians born in the industrialized West. It was a consequence of the disillusionment with parliamentary democracy, liberal convictions and the good faith of bourgeois intellectuals that resulted from the fiasco of the European revolutions of 1848–9, and from the particular conclusion drawn by Herzen that Russia, which had not suffered this revolution, might find her salvation in the undestroyed, natural socialism of the peasant *mir*. It was deeply influenced by Bakunin's violent diatribes against all forms of central authority, and in particular the state; and by his vision of men as being by nature peaceful and productive, and rendered violent only when they are perverted from their proper ends, and forced to be either gaolers or convicts. But it was also fed by the streams that flowed in a contrary direction: by Tkachev's faith in a Jacobin *élite* of professional revolutionaries as the only force capable of destroying the advance of capitalism helped on its fatal path by innocent reformists and humanitarians and careerist intellectuals, and concealed behind the repulsive sham of parliamentary democracy; even more by the passionate utilitarianism of Pisarev, and his brilliant polemics against all forms of idealism and amateurishness, and in particular the sentimental idealization of the simplicity and beauty of peasants in general, and of Russian peasants in particular, as beings touched by grace, remote from the corrupting influences of the decaying West. It was supported by the appeal which these "critical realists" made to their compatriots to save themselves by self-help and hard-headed energy — a kind of neo-Encyclopaedist campaign in favour of natural science, skill and professionalism, directed against the humanities, classical learning, history and other forms of "sybaritic" self-indulgence. Above all it contrasted "realism" with the literary culture which had lulled the best men in Russia into a condition where corrupt bureaucrats, stupid and brutal landowners and an obscurantist Church could exploit them or let them rot, while aesthetes and liberals looked the other way.

But the deepest strain of all, the very centre of the Populist outlook, was the individualism and rationalism of Lavrov and Mikhailovsky. With Herzen they believed that history followed no predetermined pattern, that it possessed "no libretto," that neither the violent conflicts between cultures, nations, classes (which for Hegelians constituted the essence of human progress) nor the struggles for power by one class over another (represented by Marxists as being the motive force of history) were inevitable. Faith in human freedom was the cornerstone of Populist humanism; the Populists never tired of repeating that ends were chosen by men, not imposed upon them, and that men's wills alone could construct a happy and honourable life — a life in which the interests of intellectuals, peasants, manual workers and the liberal professions could be reconciled; not indeed made wholly to coincide, for that was an unattainable ideal; but adjusted in an unstable equilibrium, which human reason and constant human care could adjust to the largely unpredictable consequences of the interaction of men with each other and with nature. It may be that the tradition of the Orthodox Church with its conciliar and communal principles and deep antagonism both to the authoritarian hierarchy of the Roman Church, and the individualism of the Protestants, also exercised its share of influence. These doctrines and these prophets and their Western masters — French radicals before and after the French revolution, as well as Fichte and Buonarroti, Fourier and Hegel, Mill and Proudhon, Owen and Marx, played their part. But the largest figure in the Populist movement, the man whose temperament, ideas and activities dominated it from beginning to end, is undoubtedly that of Nikolai Gavrilovich Chernyshevsky and his immediate allies and followers. The influence of his life and teachings, despite a multitude of monographs, still await its interpreter.

Nicholas Chernyshevsky was not a man of original ideas. He did not possess the depth, the imagination or the brilliant intellect and literary talent of Herzen, nor the eloquence, the boldness, the temperament or the reasoning power of Bakunin, nor the moral genius and unique social insight of Belinsky. But he was a man of unswerving integrity, immense industry and a capacity rare among Russians for concentration upon concrete detail. His deep, steady, lifelong hatred of slavery, injustice and irrationality did not express itself in large theoretical generalizations, or the creation of a sociological or metaphysical system, or violent action against authority. It took the form of slow, uninspired, patient accumulation of facts and ideas — a crude, dull but powerful intellectual structure on which one might found a detailed policy of practical action appropriate to the specific Russian environment which he desired to alter. Chernyshevsky was in greater sympathy with the concrete, carefully elaborated socialist plans, however mistaken they might be, of the Petrashevsky group (to which Dostoevsky had belonged in his youth crushed by the government in 1849), than to the great imaginative constructions of Herzen, Bakunin and their followers.

A new generation had grown up during the dead years after 1849. These young men had witnessed vacillation and outright betrayals on the part of liberals which had led to the victories of the reactionary parties in 1849. Twelve years later they saw the same phenomenon in their own country, when the manner in which the peasants had been emancipated in Russia seemed to them to be a cynical travesty of all their plans and hopes. Such men as these found the plodding genius of Chernyshevsky, his attempts to work out specific solutions to specific problems in terms of concrete statistical data; his constant appeal to facts; his patient efforts to indicate attainable, practical, immediate ends rather than desirable states of affairs to which there was no visible road; his flat, dry, pedestrian style, his very dullness and lack of inspiration, more serious and, ultimately, more inspiring than the noble flights of the romantic idealists of the 'forties. His relatively low social origin (he was the son of a parish priest) gave him a natural affinity with the humble folk whose condition he was seeking to analyse, and an abiding distrust, later to turn into fanatical hatred, of all liberal theorists, whether in Russia or the West. These qualities made Chernyshevsky a natural leader of a disenchanted generation of socially mingled origins, no longer dominated by good birth, embittered by the failure of their own early ideals, by government repression, by the humiliation of Russia in the Crimean War, by the weakness, heartlessness, hypocrisy and chaotic incompetence of the ruling class. To these tough-minded, socially insecure, angry, suspicious young radicals contemptuous of the slightest trace of eloquence or "literature," Chernyshevsky was a father and confessor, as neither the aristocratic and ironical Herzen nor the wayward and ultimately frivolous Bakunin could ever become.

Like all Populists, Chernyshevsky believed in the need to preserve the peasant commune and to spread its principles to industrial production. He believed that Russia could profit directly by learning from the scientific advances of the West, without going through the agonies of an industrial revolution. "Human development is a form of chronological unfairness," Herzen had once characteristically observed, "since late-comers are able to profit by the labours of their predecessors without paying the same price"; "History is fond of her grandchildren," Chernyshevsky repeated after him, "for it offers them the marrow of the bones, which the previous generation had hurt its hands in breaking." For Chernyshevsky history moved along a spiral, in Hegelian triads, since every generation tends to repeat the experience not of its parents, but of its grandparents, and repeats it at a "higher level." But it is not this historicist element in his doctrine that bound its spell upon the Populists. They were most of all influenced by his acute distrust of reforms from above, by his belief that the essence of history was a struggle between the classes, above all by his conviction (which derives nothing, so far as we know, from Marx, but draws upon socialist sources common to both) that the state is always the instrument of the dominant class, and cannot, whether it consciously desires this or not, embark on those necessary reforms the success of which would end its own domination. No order can be persuaded to undertake its own dissolution. Hence all attempts to influence the Tsar, all attempts to evade the horrors of revolution, must (he concluded in the early 'sixties) remain necessarily vain. There was a moment in the late 'fifties when, like Herzen, he had hoped for reforms from above. The final form of the Emancipation, and the concessions which the government had made to the landowners, cured him of this illusion. He pointed out with a good deal of historical justification that the liberals, who hoped to influence the government by Fabian tactics, thus far merely succeeded in betraying both the peasants and themselves: first they compromised themselves with the peasants by their relations with their masters; after that, the governing class found little difficulty, whenever this suited their convenience, in representing them as false friends to the peasants and turning the latter against them. This had occurred in both France and Germany in 1849. Even if the moderates withdrew in time, and advocated violent measures, their ignorance of conditions and blindness to the peasants' and workers' actual needs usually led them to advocate utopian schemes which in the end cost their followers a terrible price.

Chernyshevsky had evolved a simple form of historical materialism, according to which social factors determined political ones, and not *vice versa.* Consequently he held with Fourier and Proudhon that liberal and parliamentary ideals merely evaded the central issues: the peasants and the workers needed food, shelter, boots; as for the right to vote, or to be governed by liberal constitutions, or to obtain guarantees of personal liberty, these meant little to hungry and half-naked men. The social revolution must come first: appropriate political reforms would follow of themselves. For Chernyshevsky the principal lesson of 1848 was that the Western liberals, the brave no less than the cowardly, had demonstrated their political and moral bankruptcy, and with it that of their Russian disciples — Herzen, Kavelin, Granovsky, and the rest. Russia must pursue her own path. Unlike the Slavophils, and like the Russian Marxists of the next generation, he maintained with a wealth of economic evidence that the historical development of Russia, and in particular the peasant *mir,* were in no sense unique, but followed the social and economic laws that governed all human societies. Like the Marxists (and the Comtian positivists), he believed that such laws could be discovered and stated; but unlike the Marxists, he was convinced that by adopting Western techniques, and educating a body of men of trained and resolute wills and rational outlook, Russia could "leap over" the capitalist stage of social development, and transform her village communes and free cooperative groups of craftsmen into agricultural and industrial associations of producers who would constitute the embryo of the new socialist society. Technological progress did not, in his view, automatically break up the peasant commune: "savages can be taught to use Latin script and safety matches"; factories can be grafted on to workers' *artels* without destroying them; large-scale organization could eliminate exploitation, and yet preserve the predominantly agricultural nature of the Russian economy.*

Chernyshevsky believed in the decisive historical rôle of the application of science to life, but unlike Pisarev, did not regard individual enterprise, still less capitalism as indispensable to this process. He retained enough of the Fourierism of his youth to look upon the free associations of peasant communes and craftsmen's *artels* as the basis of all freedom and progress. But at the same time, like the Saint-Simonians, he was convinced that little would be achieved without collective action — state socialism on a vast scale. These incompatible beliefs were never reconciled; Chernyshevsky's writings contain statements both in favour of and against the desirability of large-scale industry. He is similarly ambivalent about the part to be played (and the part to be avoided) by the state as the stimulator and controller of industry, about the function of managers of large collective industrial enterprises, about the relations of the public and private sectors of the economy, and about the political sovereignty of the democratically elected parliament and its relation to the state as the source of centralized economic planning and control.

The outlines of Chernyshevsky's social programme remained vague or inconsistent, and often both. It is the concrete detail which, founded as it was on real experience, spoke directly to the representatives of the great popular masses, who had at last found a spokesman and interpreter of their own needs and feelings. His deepest aspirations and emotions were poured into *What is to be done?*, a social utopia which, grotesque as a work of art, had a literally epoch-making effect on Russian opinion. This didactic novel described the "new men" of the free, morally pure, cooperative socialist commonwealth of the future; its touching sincerity and moral passion bound their spell upon the imaginations of the idealistic and guilt-stricken sons of prosperous parents, and provided them with an ideal model in the light of which an entire generation of revolutionaries educated and hardened itself to the defiance of existing laws and conventions, and acceptance of exile and death with sublime unconcern. Chernyshevsky preached a naïve utilitarianism. Like James Mill, and perhaps Bentham, he held that basic human nature was a fixed, physiologically analysable, pattern of natural processes and faculties, and that the maximization of human happiness could therefore be scientifically planned and realized. Having decided that imaginative writing and criticism were the only available media in Russia for propagating radical ideas, he filled the *Contemporary*, a review which he edited together with the poet Nekrasov, with as high a proportion of direct socialist doctrine as could be smuggled in under the guise of literature. In this work he was helped by the violent young critic Dobrolyubov, a genuinely gifted man of letters (which Chernyshevsky was not) who, at times, went even further in his passionate desire to preach and educate. The aesthetic views of the two zealots were severely practical. Chernyshevsky laid it down that the function of art was to help men to satisfy their wants more rationally, to disseminate knowledge, to combat ignorance, prejudice

* [According to] Populist statistics (which seem plausible enough) . . . the number of peasants to that of landowners in the 'sixties was of the order of 234:1, while the land owned by them stood to that of their masters in the ratio of 1:11½, and their incomes were 2.5:97.5; as for industry, the proportion of city workers to peasants was 1:100. Given these figures it is perhaps not surprising that Marx should have declared that his prognosis applied to the Western economies, and not necessarily to that of the Russians, even though his Russian disciples ignored this concession, and insisted that capitalism was making enormous strides in Russia, and would soon obliterate the differences that divided it from the West. . . .

and the anti-social passions, to improve life in the most literal and narrow sense of these words. Driven to absurd consequences, he embraced them gladly. Thus he explained that the chief value of marine paintings was that they showed the sea to those who, like, for instance, the inhabitants of central Russia, lived too far away from it ever to see it for themselves; and he maintained that his friend and patron Nekrasov, because by his verse he moved men to greater sympathy with the oppressed than other poets had done, was for that reason the greatest Russian poet, living or dead. His earlier collaborators, civilized and fastidious men of letters like Turgenev and Botkin found this grim fanaticism increasingly difficult to bear. Turgenev could not long live with this art hating and dogmatic schoolmaster. Tolstoy despised his dreary provincialism, his total lack of aesthetic sense, his intolerance, his wooden rationalism, his maddening self-assurance. But these very qualities, or, rather, the outlook of which they were characteristic, helped to make him the natural leader of the "hard" young men who had succeeded the idealists of the 'forties. Chernyshevsky's harsh, flat, dull, humourless, grating sentences, his preoccupation with concrete economic detail, his self-discipline, his passionate dedication to the material and moral good of his fellow men, the grey, self-effacing personality, the tireless, devoted, minute industry, the hatred of style or of any concessions to the graces, the unquestionable sincerity, the combination of brutal directness, utter self-forgetfulness, indifference to the claims of private life, innocence, personal kindness, pedantry, moral charm, capacity for self-sacrifice, created the image that later became the prototype of the Russian revolutionary hero and martyr. More than any other publicist he was responsible for drawing the final line between "us" and "them." All his life he preached that there must be no compromise with "them," that the war must be fought to the death and on every front; there were no neutrals; that, so long as this war was being fought, no work could be too trivial too repulsive or too tedious for a revolutionary to perform. His personality and outlook set its seal upon two generations of Russian revolutionaries; not least upon Lenin, who admired him devotedly.

In spite of his emphasis on economic or sociological arguments, the basic approach, the tone and outlook of Chernyshevsky and of the Populists generally, is moral, and at times indeed, religious. These men believed in socialism not because it was inevitable, nor because it was effective, not even because it alone was rational, but because it was just. Concentrations of political power, capitalism, the centralized state, trampled upon the rights of men and crippled them morally and spiritually. The Populists were stern atheists, but socialism and orthodox Christian values coalesced in their minds. They shrank from the prospect of industrialism in Russia because of its brutal cost, and they disliked the West because it had paid this price too heartlessly. Their disciples, the Populist economists of the 'eighties and 'nineties, Danielson and Vorontsov, for example, for all their strictly economic arguments against the possibility of capitalism in Russia (some of which seem a good deal sounder than their Marxist opponents have represented them as being), were in the last analysis moved by moral revulsion from the sheer mass of suffering that capitalism was destined to bring, that is to say, by a refusal to pay so appalling a price, no matter how valuable the results. Their successors in the twentieth century, the Socialist-Revolutionaries, sounded the note which runs through the whole of the Populist tradition in Russia: that the purpose of social action is not the power of the state, but the welfare of the people; that to enrich the state and provide it with military and industrial power, while undermining the health, the education, the morality, the general cultural level of its citizens, was feasible but wicked. They compared the progress of the United States, where, they maintained, the welfare of the individual was paramount, with that of Prussia, where it was not. They committed themselves to the view (which goes back at least to Sismondi) that the spiritual and physical condition of the individual citizen matters more than the power of the state, so that if, as often happened, the two stood in inverse ratio to one another, the rights and welfare of the individual must come first. They rejected as historically false the proposition that only powerful states could breed good or happy citizens, and as morally unacceptable the proposition that to lose oneself in the life and welfare of his society is the highest form of self-fulfilment for the individual. Belief in the primacy of human rights over other claims is the first principle that separates pluralist from centralized societies, and welfare states, mixed economies, "New Deal" policies, from one-party governments, "closed" societies, "five-year plans," and, in general, forms of life built to serve a single goal that transcends the varied goals of differing groups or individuals. Chernyshevsky was more fanatical than his followers in the 'seventies and 'eighties, and believed far more strongly in organization, but even he neither stopped his ears to the cries for immediate help which he heard upon all sides, nor believed in the need to suppress the wants of individuals who were making desperate efforts to escape destruction, in the interests of even the most sacred and overmastering purpose. There were times when he was a narrow and unimaginative pedant, but at his worst he was never impatient nor arrogant, nor inhumane, and was perpetually reminding his readers and himself that in their zeal to help, the educators must not end by bullying their would-be beneficiaries, that what "we"— the rational intellectuals — think good for the peasants may be not what they themselves want, and that to ram "our" remedies down "their" throats is not permitted. Neither he nor Lavrov, nor even the most ruthlessly Jacobin among the proponents of terror and violence, ever took cover behind the inevitable direction of history as a justification of what would otherwise have been patently unjust or brutal. If violence was the only means to a given end, then there might be circumstances in which it was right to employ it; but this must be justified in each case by the intrinsic moral claim of the end — an increase in happiness, or solidarity, or justice, or peace, or some other universal human value that outweighs the evil of the means, never by the view that it was rational and necessary to march in step with history, ignoring one's scruples and dismissing one's own "subjective" moral principles because they were necessarily provisional, on the ground that history herself transformed all moral systems and retrospectively justified only those principles which survived and succeeded.

The mood of the Populists, particularly in the 'seventies, can fairly be described as religious. This group of conspirators or propagandists saw itself, and was seen by others, as constituting a dedicated order. The first condition of membership was the sacrifice of one's entire life to the movement, both to the particular group and party, and to the cause of the revolution in general. But the notion of the dictatorship of the party or of its leaders over individual lives — in particular over the beliefs of individual revolutionaries — is no part of this doctrine, and is indeed contrary to its entire spirit. The only censor over the individual's acts is his individual conscience. If one has promised obedience to the leaders of the party, such an oath is sacred, but it extends only to the specific revolutionary objectives of the party and not beyond them, and ends with the completion of whatever specific goals the party exists to promote — in the last resort, the revolution. Once the revolution has been made, each individual is free to act as he thinks right, since discipline is a temporary means and not an end. The Populists did indeed virtually invent the conception of the party as a group of professional conspirators with no private lives, obeying a total discipline — the core of the "hard" professionals, as against mere sympathizers and fellow-travellers; but this sprang from the specific situation that obtained in Tsarist Russia, and the necessity, and conditions for effective conspiracy, and not from belief in hierarchy as a form of life desirable or even tolerable in itself. Nor did the conspirators justify their acts by appealing to a cosmic process which sanctified their every act, since they believed in freedom of human choice and not in determinism. The later Leninist conception of the revolutionary party and its dictatorship, although historically it owed much to these trained martyrs of an earlier day, sprang from a different outlook. The young men who poured into the villages during the celebrated summer of 1874, only to meet with non-comprehension, suspicion and often outright hostility on the part of the peasants, would have been profoundly astonished and indignant if they had been told that they were to look upon themselves as the sacred instruments of history, and that their acts were therefore to be judged by a moral code different from that common to other men.

The Populist movement was a failure. "Socialism bounced off people like peas from a wall," wrote the celebrated terrorist Stepnyak Kravchinsky to his fellow revolutionary Vera Zasulich in 1876, two years after the original wave of enthusiasm had died down. "They listen to our people as they do to the priest" — respectfully, without understanding, without any effect upon their actions. "There is noise in the capitals /The prophets thunder/A furious war of words is waged/But in the depths, in the heart of Russia,/There all is still, there is ancient peace." These lines by Nekrasov convey the mood of frustration which followed the failure of the sporadic efforts made by the revolutionary idealists in the late 'sixties and early 'seventies, peaceful propagandists and isolated terrorists alike — of whom Dostoevsky painted so violent a picture in *The Possessed*. The government caught these men, exiled them, imprisoned them, and by its obstinate unwillingness to promote any measures to alleviate the consequences of an inadequate land reform drove liberal opinion towards sympathy with the revolutionaries. They felt that public opinion was on their side, and finally resorted to organized terrorism. Yet their ends always remained moderate enough. The open letter which they addressed to the new Emperor in 1881 is mild and liberal in tone. "Terror," said the celebrated revolutionary Vera Figner many years later, "was intended to create opportunities for developing the faculties of men for service to society." The society for which violence was to blast the way was to be peaceful, tolerant, decentralized and humane. The principal enemy was still the state.

The wave of terrorism reached its climax with the assassination of Alexander II in 1881. The hoped-for revolution did not break out. The revolutionary organizations were crushed, and the new Tsar decided upon a policy of extreme repression. In this he was, on the whole, supported by public opinion, which recoiled before the assassination of an Emperor who had, after all, emancipated the peasants, and who was said to have been meditating other liberal measures. The most prominent leaders of the movement were executed or exiled; lesser figures escaped abroad, and the most gifted of those who were still free — Plekhanov and Akselrod — gradually moved towards Marxism. They felt embarrassed by Marx's own concession that Russia could in principle avoid passing through a capitalist stage even without the aid of a communist world revolution — a thesis which Engels conceded far more grudgingly and with qualifications — and maintained that Russia had in fact already entered the capitalist stage. They declared that, since the development of capitalism in Russia was no more avoidable than it had been in its day in the West, nothing was to be gained by averting one's face from the "iron" logic of history, and that for these reasons, so far from resisting industrialization, socialists should encourage it, indeed profit by the fact that it, and it alone, could breed the army of revolutionaries which would be sufficient to overthrow the capitalist enemy — an army to be formed out of the growing city proletariat, organized and disciplined by the very conditions of its labour.

The vast forward leap in industrial development made by Russia in the 'nineties seemed to support the Marxist thesis. It proved attractive to revolutionary intellectuals for many reasons: because it claimed to be founded on a scientific analysis of the laws of history which no society could hope to evade; because it claimed to be able to "prove" that, although much violence, misery and injustice — exploitation, pauperization, conflicts between classes, nations, interests — were bound to occur as the pattern of history inexorably unfolded itself, yet the story would have a happy ending. Hence the conscience of those who felt guilty because they acquiesced in the miseries of the workers, or at any rate did not take active — that is, violent — steps to alleviate or prevent them, as Populist policy had demanded, felt assuaged by the "scientific" guarantee that the road, covered though it might be with the corpses of the innocent, led inevitably to the gates of an earthly paradise. According to this view the expropriators would find themselves expropriated by the sheer logic of human development, although the course of history might be shortened, and the birth pangs made easier, by conscious organization, and above all an increase in knowledge (that is, education) on the part of the workers and their leaders. This was particularly welcome to those who, understandably reluctant to continue with useless terrorism which merely led to Siberia or the scaffold, now found doctrinal justification for peaceful study and the life of ideas, which the intellectuals among them found far more congenial than bomb-throwing.

The heroism, the disinterestedness, the personal nobility of the Populists, was often admitted by their Marxist opponents. They were regarded as worthy forerunners of a truly rational revolutionary party, and Chernyshevsky was sometimes accorded an even higher status and was credited with insights of genius — an empirical and unscientific, but instinctively correct, approach to truths of which only Marx and Engels could provide the demonstration, armed as they were with the instrument of an exact science to which neither Chernyshevsky, nor any other Russian thinker of his day, had yet attained. Marx and Engels grew to be particularly indulgent to the Russians: they were praised for having done wonders for amateurs, remote from the West and using home-made tools; they alone in Europe had, by 1880, created a truly revolutionary situation in their country; but it was made clear, particularly by Kautsky, that this was no substitute for professional methods and the use of the new machinery provided by scientific socialism. Populism was written down as an amalgam of unorganized moral indignation and utopian ideas in the muddled heads of self-taught peasants, well-meaning university intellectuals and other social casualties of the confused interim between the end of an obsolescent feudalism and the beginning of the new capitalist phase in a backward country. Marxist historians still tend to describe it as a movement compounded of systematic misinterpretation of economic facts and social realities, noble but useless individual terrorism, and spontaneous or ill-directed peasant risings — the necessary but pathetic beginnings of real revolutionary activity, the prelude to the real play, a scene of naïve ideas and frustrated practice destined to be swept away by the new revolutionary, dialectical science heralded by Plekhanov and Lenin.

What were the ends of Populism? Violent disputes took place about means and methods, about timing, but not about ultimate purposes. Anarchism, equality, a full life for all, these were universally accepted. It is as if the entire movement — the motley variety of revolutionary types . . . — Jacobins and moderates, terrorists and educators, Lavrists and Bakuninists, "troglodytes," "recalcitrants" and "country folk," members of "Land and Liberty" and of "The People's Will," were all dominated by a single myth: that once the monster was slain, the sleeping princess — the Russian peasantry — would awaken and without further ado live happily for ever after.

Lenin: Proletarian Revolution Has to Be Made Inevitable

ALFRED G. MEYER

A Professor of Political Science at Michigan State University, Alfred Meyer is one of the West's distinguished analysts of Marxian and Leninist thought and of Soviet Communism as it has developed since 1917. He has concentrated his scholarly life upon the study of these subjects, as is demonstrated by his books: *Marxism* (1954), *Leninism* (1957), and *Communism* (1960). Together with Gustav Hilger he has also written *The Incompatible Allies: A Memoir History of German-Soviet Relations* (1953). In the following extract from *Leninism,* Professor Meyer describes the singularly important developments of Lenin's thought that were provoked by the revolution of 1905. For the student seeking to comprehend the roles played by Lenin and his Bolshevik Party after 1905, it is essential to understand the decisions Lenin came to after living through this first Russian revolution of the twentieth century.

I

When Lenin called himself a Marxist it meant, to him, that he had accepted the axiom of the moral and actual inevitability of the proletarian revolution. In his eyes, the acid test of a Marxist was his unceasing striving toward this revolution. This revolution was seen as a political act, the seizure of power by the leaders of the proletariat, so that the establishment of a proletarian dictatorship was Lenin's guiding aim.

* * *

And what kind of revolution was it to be? It could not very well be expected that a proletarian revolution in Russia, or any revolution whatsoever, would usher in the socialist society predicted by Marx and Engels. Russia's grain-producing peasant society could not be expected to produce that abundance of industrial products which is, according to Marxist theory, one of the essential preconditions of socialism. Hence even a proletarian revolution in Russia would have to have different results from those expected in western Europe. It might, perhaps, be viewed as a contributory development in the broader perspectives of a world-wide revolution. In any event, a Marxist in Russia was forced to think about the role that a peasant country like his own might play in the Marxist scheme.

To the question, "Who is to make revolution in Russia?" Lenin's first answer would have been, "proletarians and bourgeois intellectuals." But Lenin very early recognized that there were other classes or groups in Russian society who might become interested in making a revolution. Such groups might not share the ultimate aims of the Marxist movement, but they would be interested in change, they would be forces of unrest, negation, destruction. And, since the destruction of the old order would have to precede or accompany the construction of the new, Lenin was keenly interested in all such forces of destruction, and tried to ally his party with them. His appraisal of these forces, however, underwent periodic changes, and we shall therefore consider his analysis of the role various classes in Russia would play and of their usefulness to the cause of revolution. We shall furthermore trace the changes in Lenin's ideas on the nature of the revolution that could or would or should be made with these available forces.

As Lenin surveyed the Russian social scene in the last decade of the nineteenth century, he came to the conclusion that Marx had been right in his analysis of historic trends, and that his findings were applicable not only to western Europe but also to Russia. In the light of Russia's peculiarities, this conclusion is surprising. We should note, however, that Lenin was not alone in this opinion: the entire Marxist movement, which had struck its first feeble roots in such alien soil in the 1880's, was based on this idea. . . .

In a process which we cannot treat in this book, the Russian Marxist movement originated within, and in opposition to, the Narodniks and won its first spurs in fighting against them. The outstanding theoretician leading this fight was Georgi V. Plekhanov, whose vigorous preaching of orthodox Marxism, "scientific socialism," was directed sharply, even mercilessly, against Narodnik ideas. Inspired by Plekhanov, Lenin, too, began to develop his ideas in writing anti-Narodnik tracts. In these pamphlets he insisted that Russia was not different from the West and that the development of industrial capitalism as outlined by Marx was the path which Russia, too, was about to take. The Great Reforms, he asserted, had irreversibly transformed Russia into a bourgeois society with all its familiar contradictions and its irresistible drift toward the proletarian revolution. In his very first publication he asserted that there had already been two distinct stages in Russia's capitalist development: the Great Reforms, which, he claimed, opened the way for capitalist social relationships and for the entire superstructural array that accompanies them; and capitalism, which, ever since the early nineties, had been the dominant mode of production in Russia. The political form of Russian society, he wrote, was the "class state." His principal economic work, completed in 1899, was devoted to a thorough examination of the rapid development of capitalism in Russia, both in the cities and in agriculture.

In this very work, however, Lenin showed his awareness of the relative importance that agriculture held in the Russian economy. Consequently, even though he claimed that the Marxist sociology of capitalism applied to Russia, he could not fail to observe that his country showed certain peculiar traits of its own. Indeed, Lenin did take into account the fact that the predominance of the peasantry in Russia's economy would necessitate changes in the Marxist sociology there. In a purely capitalist economy, he wrote in 1899, there are, indeed, only two classes, the bourgeoisie and the proletariat. The former possess capital and use it for the exploitation of the labor of others; the latter, constituting the great majority of people, possess nothing but their labor power and are therefore obliged to sell it to the capitalists in order to make a living. Before capitalism develops fully, however, a precapitalist bastard class continues to exist, the petty bourgeoisie, and a country's relative backwardness expresses itself in the prevalence of petty bourgeois elements.

In his early years Lenin attempted to reconcile the prevalence of the petty bourgeoisie with his characterization of Russia as a capitalist society by regarding (and virtually dismissing) the peasantry as a phenomenon belonging to the past, hence doomed to disappear before long. In viewing the peasantry and assessing its role, Lenin thus projected "inevitable" future developments into the present and based his strategy on this futuristic analysis of Russian society. In his eyes the peasantry was a dying class, which was rapidly being split into two sections, a small minority of capitalist farmers and a vast majority of rural paupers. True enough, he saw revolutionary dynamism in these paupers, but only because their pauperization was transforming them into proletarians, in the classical Marxist sense of the word. Only the peasant who had become conscious of his transformation into a proletarian interested Lenin.

In fact, Lenin's bitterness against the Narodniks stemmed from his opinion that they prevented the peasantry from becoming aware of its proletarian destiny, by maintaining that it was a class in its own right, and not a doomed one, either. Lenin thought that the Narodniks were delaying the growth of consciousness in the peasantry. In addition to fighting against their preachings, he proposed practical measures to attract "those elements of the petty bourgeoisie which gravitate toward the proletariat." This does not mean that he proposed to make concessions to them, by, for example, incorporating some of their typical demands and aspirations in his party platform. On the contrary, Lenin before 1905 believed that he could, instead, instill proletarian consciousness into the peasantry by a process of education. This was not to be accomplished by lectures or pamphlets alone; in his opinion, only hard facts that are seen and felt and resented will stimulate men's minds. The educational method he proposed was therefore the active promotion of class war in the village. He wanted to sharpen the antagonism between rich peasants and rural paupers; he wanted to show the poor that their old methods of resistance were useless, to demonstrate to them that their plight was a consequence of growth of capitalism in Russia. Thus he hoped to convince them that the proletarian revolution alone promised them a better deal. He wrote in 1902,

> We recognize the class struggle as the central fact in Russia's agrarian order. We build our entire agrarian policy (and, consequently, also our agrarian program) on the straightforward recognition of that fact with all the consequences evolving from it. Our principal and next aim is to clear the road for the free development of class war in the village, the class war of the proletariat that is directed toward the realization of the final goal of the world's social democracy, toward the conquest of political power by the proletariat and toward the creation of the basis for a socialist society. . . .

The political program corresponding to this was a fight for radical democracy. . . . Lenin saw the function of liberal democratic institutions in Russia to be, not helping the proletariat come to power, but facilitating and accelerating Russia's westernization. His cry for democracy was a measure of warfare against the old order, the tsarist dynasty, its bureaucratic state apparatus, the privileged, land-owning gentry, the army, and the police. All these classes, persons, and institutions were considered by Lenin to be the last obstacles in Russia's road to a capitalist society. Or rather, he asserted that this transformation had already taken place; it was merely obscured by the tsarist political structure. Hence he could write: "In order to clear the road for the free development of class warfare in the village, it is necessary to remove all remnants of the feudal order which are at present *covering up* the beginnings of capitalist antagonism within the rural population and are preventing them from developing." Political action was thus seen as the midwife who could tear the new society from the womb of old institutions. Superstructural means, to use Marxian parlance, would help to reveal substructural change. "The fight of the Russian working class for its liberation is a political fight," Lenin wrote as early as 1895, "and its first objective is the achievement of political liberty."

In consequence, Lenin called on the proletariat to support all liberal parties in the fight for political liberty. His minimum program, in these years, was to bring about what he called the bourgeois revolution in Russia. It therefore consisted of demands for universal, direct, equal, and secret elections, for political and civil liberties, for the liberation of the peasantry from the inequalities imposed by the Great Reforms, and also for a certain amount of social legislation. Lenin's minimum program up to 1905 was thoroughly liberal: he expressly warned against any open emphasis being placed on socialist long-range aims, and against a flippant attitude toward the minimum objectives. He argued that any admission by his followers that liberal democracy was only the minimum aim would lead them to half-heartedness in supporting these demands. Speaking about a draft for a party platform that was being discussed, he wrote, "It is fully sufficient if we say that the autocracy is retarding or repressing 'the *entire* social development': that means that it is incompatible also with the development of capitalism." This caution on Lenin's part reveals the value he placed on the alliance of his party with other enemies of tsarist autocracy, be they peasants, bourgeois, or even members of the gentry. In his eyes, his principal allies in these years were the representatives of the bourgeoisie; this class, he thought (as did all other Russian Marxists at the time) shared with the proletariat a deep and irreconcilable hostility to the tsarist order. Yet because the bourgeoisie was in addition the natural enemy of the working class, it could not be fully trusted. True enough, according to the Marxist scheme of development it was the natural desire of the business world to bring about the so-called bourgeois revolution. But at the same time the existence of an even more revolutionary class tended to make the middle class afraid of revolutionary action, and thus prone to betray "its own" revolution.

All these arguments were familiar to Russian Marxists, and were quite generally accepted by them. There was no agreement, however, concerning the consequences to be drawn from these considerations. One school of thought might be characterized roughly as follows: The next revolution which has to be fought in Russia is the bourgeois revolution; the principal force that will fight it is the bourgeoisie. The bourgeoisie will fight it more enthusiastically if it is not at the same time troubled by forces further to the left. For this reason, the proletariat should refrain from disturbing the bourgeoisie in its fight against autocracy; it should not by its radical slogans frighten the middle class into becoming counterrevolutionary. Instead, it should lie low until the bourgeoisie has played its revolutionary role to the very end. One group, the so-called Legal Marxists, went so far as to imply that the proletariat should refrain from playing any active, or at least any leading, role in the coming bourgeois revolution. These Legal Marxists emphasized the constructive goals capitalism still had to fulfill in Russia. They warned against premature revolutionary struggles and premature political action of any sort, lest capitalism be prevented from coming to its full flowering. This fear of political action led directly to "economism," the ideology of a moderate Marxist group that succeeded the Legal Marxists. They proposed outright to let the bourgeoisie fight its own political revolution; the proletariat, meanwhile, should restrict its activities to trade-unionism and other attempts to improve its economic conditions.

Lenin's conclusions were different. True, he too maintained that the proletariat should for the time being forget its maximum objectives, but it should do so only in order to pursue its minimum aim, the bourgeois revolution, with the greatest vigor. This vigor was essential precisely because the bourgeoisie was likely to betray "its own" revolution. As a matter of fact, Lenin almost from the beginning argued that the bourgeoisie would turn counterrevolutionary no matter what the proletariat did, while attempts on the part of the workers to appease the middle class would only promote reactionary measures. Conversely, the radical spirit of the proletariat would act as the prime mover of revolutionary developments. When the most revolutionary class began to march toward its goal, it would set all other classes into motion. The action of the proletariat would thus be the spark that would touch off the bourgeois revolution.

This "theory of the spark" is a typically Leninist way of arguing, which we shall see applied in other fields later. It can be regarded as a substitute for the rigid determinism of "orthodox" Marxism. In Lenin's eyes, such determinism leads to political inaction, because it implies that the revolution will develop by its own inner dynamics without having to be promoted, and that vigorous action by the proletarian movement might only spoil its chances. Lenin's attitude of distrust is in sharp contrast to this. He was always swimming against the current, but, as a Marxist, he still needed a determinist rationale for doing so. The theory of the spark, probably little more than an optimistic myth with hardly any basis in reality, provided this for him. That the theory of the spark ("the activity of the working class will set the bourgeoisie in motion to make the bourgeois revolution") is in direct contradiction to Lenin's fears that the bourgeoisie, fearing socialism more than reaction, would be ready to betray "their own" revolution should be obvious. Both arguments were adduced to support his demand that the proletariat should undertake the role of leading the bourgeois revolution. In subsequent pages we shall see further instances of Lenin's tendency to use mutually contradicting arguments to support his policies.

To sum up: Lenin in the years around the turn of the century showed an intense hatred of tsarist autocracy and an equally intense impatience with the Russian peasant. With a very guarded faith in the revolutionary potential of the bourgeoisie, he proposed that the working class lead it and even the liberal gentry in the bourgeois revolution, which would "bring out" the capitalist nature of Russian society in its clear and naked reality. His main hatred was directed, first, against those Marxists who warned the proletariat against premature revolutionary activity, and second, against the Narodniks, who were, he thought, confusing the peasants about their inevitable destiny and thus retarding their evolution toward consciousness. We shall see that, in the period following the Revolution of 1905, Lenin changed both his analysis of the political constellation and his program of action.

II

Lenin's reaction to the Revolution of 1905 provides a good case study of his operating procedure in applying and reformulating his revolutionary strategy. . . .

In the early months of 1905, as the revolution began to develop and gather momentum, Lenin, then living in exile in western Europe, attempted to explain the events he learned about through the press by previously developed theorems, and to formulate programmatic slogans. His first impression was that the events in Russia were fully confirming his past analysis and prognosis. He therefore concluded that the situation called for pursuing his long-advocated strategy with new vigor — the time for the bourgeois revolution had finally ripened. The bourgeoisie was on the march, and the proletariat was showing them the way.

But in the summer of 1905 Lenin thought he saw signs that the revolutionary enthusiasm of the liberal bourgeoisie was lagging, after the tsar had made a number of empty promises of reform. He was not, however, easily discouraged. He maintained that the interests of the middle class could not but come in conflict with the old regime, and that this conflict would be sharper the longer it was retarded. Hence he concluded confidently that the revolution would end in the downfall of tsarism and the establishment of bourgeois democracy, if only the proletariat kept on leading all other elements of discontent in revolutionary radicalism. The proletariat, he wrote, must be the class that chooses the moment for action after gathering around it as many forces as it can. When these forces of revolution are at the peak of their organization and consciousness, and when the enemy is at his weakest, then the population must rise in revolt, and tsarism will collapse. "At that moment the proletariat will rise at the head of the revolt in order to win liberty for the entire people, and to guarantee to the working class the possibility of an open and broad struggle for socialism, a struggle which will be enriched with all of Europe's experience."

With that phrase we are reminded by Lenin that behind the minimum program of the bourgeois revolution there stands the maximum program of the proletarian class struggle and the proletarian revolution. The relationship between these programs, in Lenin's mind, was this: the closer the party comes to accomplishing the minimum program, the more actively its leaders have to think about the maximum aims. The closer democracy comes, the more it must be used for the purpose of revealing its bourgeois character. The faster the bourgeois revolution progresses, and broader masses participate in it, the more should a Marxist remember the special aims of his movement, the more aloof he should keep himself. Lenin therefore called for tighter organization, firmer class consciousness, and the jealous maintenance of the party's independence within the whole movement for bourgeois democracy. In other words, the development of the revolution caused him to move away from the idea of an alliance with liberalism, and later led him to a complete break with the liberals that could never be healed.

Meanwhile, his attitude toward the peasantry underwent an even more decided change. In February of 1905 Lenin received his first news about widespread peasant disturbances, but he did not feel compelled thereby to make alterations in his analysis of the situation. In his pamphlets and letters he welcomed the revolutionary peasants as a friendly force, as long as they were joining the fight against tsarism, but he categorically refused to support the peasants' aspirations toward the division of the gentry's land among themselves. The proletariat, he wrote, has not the slightest interest in supporting the formation of a new class of capitalist farmers in Russia; this would only mean the replacement of one type of capitalism by another. "We must," he wrote, "stand firm on our own proletarian class point of view: we must organize the rural proletariat as we do the urban, and combine them in an independent class party. We must explain to the peasants the hostile clash of their interests with those of the bourgeois peasantry and must call them to battle for the socialist revolution. We must show them that salvation from oppression and misery lies, not in the transformation of some parts of the peasantry into petty bourgeois, but in the replacement of the entire bourgeois order by a socialist one."

Two developments caused Lenin to rethink his policies. One was the proclamation of the October Manifesto, and the reaction of the liberal bourgeoisie to it. The other was the intensification of the peasants' revolutionary activity, and the highly imaginative way the tsarist government dealt with it. The first of these developments led Lenin to reappraise the role and reliability of the bourgeoisie in the bourgeois revolution, and to make corresponding changes in his political and organizational program. The second was responsible for his changed attitude toward the Russian peasantry.

In the Manifesto of 30 October 1905, Nicholas II promised his people to establish a representative assembly, called the Duma, which was to have a positive function in the legislative process. An extended franchise was to make the Duma a truly representative body, and granting the customary civil liberties was to make Russia a more democratic state. The publication of this manifesto marks the turning point of the Revolution of 1905. That Lenin sensed this very well is apparent from his comments at the time. But despite this awareness he was not yet ready to admit that the revolution had been defeated. Instead, he urged new and more vigorous revolutionary action, and heartily supported the last-ditch effort of the revolution in December of 1905, when the working class went on strike on a mass scale and fought on barricades in the streets of Moscow. This uprising was suppressed by the guards regiments recently returned from the front, and Lenin had to admit that, at least for the time being, the revolution had passed its peak. It was obvious to him that the proletariat had gone to the barricades too late. The moment of the enemy's greatest weakness and of the masses' greatest enthusiasm had been missed. Immediately the Moscow uprising became the focus of heated debates between the two wings of the Russian Marxist movement. The moderates denounced it as a desperate and foolish adventure, while Lenin heatedly defended it, accusing the moderates of timidity and opportunism.

At the same time, Lenin considered the reasons for the failure of the uprising. What, he asked, had changed the mood of the country before the workers of Moscow delivered their blows? His answer was that the October Manifesto, by appeasing some and neutralizing other factions within the Russian bourgeoisie, had transformed it into a defender of the new *status quo*. Two liberal parties formed as a result of the October Manifesto, a conservative group, the Octobrists, who united on the basis of complete satisfaction with the concessions made, and a left-wing opposition, the Constitutional Democrats ("Cadets"), who accepted the reforms as a working compromise that might serve as a basis from which to fight for further gradual reforms. Viewing these developments, Lenin declared that the bourgeoisie had forsaken its own revolution and had turned into His Majesty's Loyal Opposition. It had lost all significance in the revolutionary struggle that constituted Lenin's minimum program. He had never denied the possibility of such a development, but his strategy had up to that time been based, nonetheless, on the more optimistic belief that the bourgeoisie was compelled by historical necessity to fight for radical democracy. This belief he now abandoned, arguing that the bourgeoisie had sold its services to the counterrevolution for the mere semblance of a constitution. Soon he was to maintain that it could not have been otherwise; in 1908 he stated, "The fact is that the group which in Europe constituted the core of revolutionary democracy — urban guild handicraft, the urban bourgeoisie and petty bourgeoisie — *had to* turn toward counterrevolutionary liberalism in Russia." Nor was he at a loss to explain the reasons: the pressure of international capital and the Russian middle class's fear of the masses. In 1915, he wrote:

> We Bolsheviks have always said, especially since the spring of 1906, that the Cadets and Octobrists represent the liberal bourgeoisie as a *united* force. The decade from 1905 to 1915 has confirmed our view. In the decisive moments of the struggle, Cadets and Octobrists together have betrayed democracy and have gone to help the tsar and the landlords. . . . The international setting of the Russian revolution as well as the strength of the proletariat have made that behavior of the liberals inevitable.

After 1905, Lenin was quick to draw the political consequences of this situation as he saw it. The tenuous and uneasy alliance which "the proletariat" (meaning, his party) had made, however unilaterally, with the liberals was now canceled, and open class war with the bourgeoisie was the slogan he advanced. Further, a new aspect was added to his views concerning the usefulness of democracy in the proletariat's class struggle. Until 1905 he had, however vaguely, subscribed to the view that the working class might very well come to power by legal means, given political democracy, though he did not trouble to point out precisely what circumstances might favor a revolution by consent. In any event, democracy had, somehow, been considered to be the normal transitional stage between tsarism and the proletarian revolution; it would take the form of a constitutional republic that might function smoothly for an undefined historical period. Should it function well, it might give the proletariat a chance to seize power by legal means. The acceptance of the October compromise by the liberal bourgeoisie, followed by twelve years of tsarist constitutionalism, gave this vague optimism a severe blow. As we have seen, Lenin continued to fight for the extension of democratic rights and institutions. But we also saw that the word "democracy" gradually acquired a different meaning. It no longer connoted a relatively stable regime in which the classes might muster their forces for new revolutionary battles, using both constitutional and unconstitutional means. Democracy meant now the acute dissolution not only of the old regime but also of capitalist society. It would be achieved only at the moment when civil war between the two main classes had broken out. . . .

THE LIBERALS

The Liberals Before 1905: Oscillation Between "Small Deeds" and "Senseless Dreams"

GEORGE FISCHER

Professor of Government at Cornell University, George Fischer was born in Berlin, completed his early education in Russia and received his Ph.D. from Harvard University. He is the author of two excellent books: *Soviet Opposition to Stalin* (1952) and *Russian Liberalism* (1958). In the latter work, an extract of which appears below, Professor Fischer has performed a valuable service by explaining the role of the hard-to-define Russian liberal after 1861 and by tracing the way in which the gentry liberals eventually joined with a newly developed liberal intelligentsia in the cities to form a real, if equivocal, force in the Russian politics of the early twentieth century.

I

NOT only did Russian autocracy tolerate the press as a substitute for institutionalized politics outside the state, but during the Great Reforms of the 1860's the autocracy itself created the outstanding new arena: local self-government. In this arena Russian liberalism focused its politics after the Great Reforms, and here the "small deeds" liberal notables were most active between the 1860's and the 1890's.

Both before and after the Great Reforms, these liberal notables — the independently wealthy dilettanti in politics — emanated from the nobility. But there was a difference. In the earlier period, the liberals stressed emancipation of the serfs. This isolated them from their own class and meant that liberalism then was confined to individual writing and theorizing. The only larger ventures were Nikolai Novikov's short-lived Enlightenment campaign through Freemasonry, at the end of the eighteenth century, and the still briefer semiliberal conspiracy of the Decembrists. Only after the Great Reforms did the liberals operate not against the nobility but within one of its segments, the gentry.[1]

It was no mere accident that after the Great Reforms the gentry was for many years the major source of Russian liberal-

[1] Technically, the term "gentry" is synonymous with "nobility," that is, a landowning class with some hereditary privilege. But in Russia, as elsewhere in Europe, the nobility tended to divide into two parts according to origin and to function. With respect to origin, a more ancient nobility, once sovereign and hence aristocratic, was in early modern times augmented by a service nobility created by the rising monarchs. In terms of function, the service nobility inclined toward military service, local administration, and smaller landowning, while the aristocracy oscillated between high office in the central state and their own large estates. As a result, in common parlance, and in this study as well, "gentry" refers to the new lesser squirearchy, and "aristocracy" to the numerically slight older and higher nobility.

ism. Education, worldliness, and access to the state made the nobility the only class in nineteenth-century Russia that dared engage in politics. The one other potential source of independently wealthy notables, the business "bourgeoisie," did not. Neither did the aristocratic segment of the nobility, since large estates and in particular high government offices bound it more tightly to the state and the *status quo*. The gentry had the aristocracy's qualifications for leadership without most of its economic and career advantages.

Furthermore, the gentry never quite adjusted economically to the revolution in Russian agriculture caused by the freeing of serfs in the Emancipation of 1861. Large-scale capitalist farming, then becoming fashionable in Russia, was beyond its means — and clashed with its anti-business traditions, which were reminiscent of the French nobility. The world agricultural crisis of the 1870's, which in Russia lingered on until the end of the century, made matters still worse. A last blow came in the 1890's, when the favoritism of industry became official state policy. As a result, the whole of the nobility lost its landholdings at a disastrous rate, one third of them in the last three decades of the nineteenth century and half by 1905.

A mood of despondency resulted, and a hearty dislike for the government's professional administrators, the "bureaucracy," which was blamed most often for the nobility's and the country's ailments. It would be wrong, however, to conclude that the Russian gentry was therefore ripe for political opposition. For the gentry, like the whole nobility, was a class that a strong state had pampered for centuries with economic advantages, social privileges, government offices. This age-long process, accompanied by increased political impotence and dependence on the state, made a *Fronde* far less likely than its opposite. In common with the Russian aristocracy, the gentry preferred continued patronage to political action outside the state, against the state.

Yet the economic crisis was unmistakable; the officials' ascendancy offended the nobility's rarely asserted claims to elite status; there was fear of revolution from below and of favoritism of industry from above. Thus a subtle change did take place after the Great Reforms in this economically insolvent, politically impotent, but socially and financially still pampered gentry. On occasion it could now as a group relish — within the narrow limits of the unsubversive and the uncontroversial — the plaints of its liberals against "the bureaucracy," their pleas for agriculture and local autonomy. That this *rapprochement* endured is explainable only by the coincidence of two different developments: on the one hand, the large antiliberal segment of the gentry had temporarily withdrawn from public affairs, and, on the other, all the more or less oppositional elements of the whole class were now syphoned and concentrated in one institution — the new self-government.

II

Initiated in 1864 for the countryside, this new institution of local self-government was designated the *zemstvo* after ancient Russian usage. Like Prussia's comparable *Landtag,* this word may best be translated as "territorial assembly."

The zemstvo was the most extensive and autonomous form of self-government in Russian history. Peter the Great and half a century later Catherine II had made gestures in this direction. But the resulting schemes centered on separate corporate organizations of different estates or classes. And they were sickly growths that did not lead to any new tradition of independence or initiative in relation to the paternalistic central government. The zemstvo was to be "all-class" (*vsesoslovnoe*), composed of elected representatives of all estates, and its jurisdiction was larger than that of the earlier schemes.

Some three dozen provinces in European Russia were allowed by the government to establish zemstvos, the less Russian areas all being excluded. These provinces (*guberniia*) were broken up into approximately

400 smaller districts (*uezd*). In both provinces and districts, the zemstvo consisted of two bodies: (1) an assembly of delegates (*glasnye*), which met annually and was elected for three-year terms; and (2) a permanent, salaried executive body, the zemstvo board, whose members were elected by the respective zemstvo assemblies, likewise for a three-year term.

The electorate of the zemstvo comprised three separate categories: the towns, the peasant communes, and all individual landowners, including non-nobility. Representation was proportional to land ownership, which meant that urban representation was sparse. The constituency elected the delegates to the lower, district assemblies by indirect methods. In the case of the peasant communes, the already existing canton (*volost*) councils elected the delegates, while the landowners chose electoral colleges for the same purpose. Delegates to the higher, province assemblies were elected by the district zemstvo assemblies from among their own members, regardless of class. In the first set of elections, during the 1860's, the number of district delegates totaled almost 12,000 and that of province delegates, over 2,000. More than 1,200 members of zemstvo boards were also elected.

From the outset, the nobility — and its most numerous group, the gentry — predominated in the zemstvo. Nor was this surprising. Even before the Great Reforms, the nobility had enjoyed a near-monopoly of local offices. Afterward, it continued to be the most privileged class in local as in national affairs. By the zemstvo statute of 1864 each marshal of the nobility, an influential local leftover of Catherine II's corporate self-government, became the ex officio chairman of his district or province zemstvo assembly. Peasant electors were free to choose their delegates from other classes, and occasionally — sometimes with outside pressure — they elected landowners. Above all, education, self-confidence, and social status gave the nobility a pre-eminence that neither the peasantry nor the small town bourgeoisie in the zemstvo ever sought to challenge.

Statistics dramatize the nobility's hegemony, showing that the nobility as a whole held 42 per cent of the district assembly seats, and that it was still more numerous in the province assemblies (74 per cent) and in zemstvo boards (62 per cent) where estates did not vote separately, as they did in the lower, district assemblies. Over the years, the gentry's hold over the zemstvo remained so strong that it retained the same percentage of district seats for three decades, although during that period (1860's–1890's) its landholdings shrank by almost one third.

What were the functions of this novel institution, dominated as it was by the nobility? The zemstvo had partial or complete jurisdiction over several areas of local rural life:

Education — particularly primary schooling. The zemstvo shared this leading concern with the Ministry of Public Education, the parochial schools, and the peasant communes. The building and maintenance of schools were augmented by the zemstvo through the training of teachers, preparation of textbooks, and adult vocational courses for peasants on agronomy, machinery, and the like.

Welfare — above all health, through a network of hospitals, dispensaries, first-aid stations; also life and fire insurance, veterinary service, saving banks, famine relief, soil conservation.

Administration — the maintenance and construction of local roads, assistance to prisons and postal services, elaborate statistical surveys.

Before the Great Reforms, before the 1860's, many of these activities had been controlled by the individual nobleman-landowner in his manorial jurisdiction over his serfs. Most of the remainder had been vested in the nobility's own units of self-government. Still others had been part of the government apparatus — or had not been organized at all. Now all these innumerable local activities converged in a new institution subject to popularly elected representatives and officers. This was indeed one of the major transformations of recent Russian history. It is not surprising that the enthusiastic expectations of some were soon matched by bitter opposition from others in the gentry and also in the government.

"Ambivalent" probably best describes the government's attitude toward its own recent progeny. As an entirely new form of rural self-government, the zemstvo was bound to arouse the expectation, joyous or apprehensive, that from the local level it might expand to the national, that it would be the "building" to which a parliament would be the logical "roof." In the deliberations before 1864, such hopes were voiced by Alexander II himself and by a number of high officials. Ere long, the "building-roof" analogy of a zemstvo structure capped by a parliament became ubiquitous in constitutionalist thought and in its agitational appeals. The government's own plans originally gave the zemstvo sweeping autonomy and jurisdiction, but as early as 1864, when the new self-government was officially promulgated, the tide had turned and a countercurrent had set in. Although the original scheme was not dropped, it was modified here and there. Where previously the zemstvo was to enjoy a minor share of politics and even of power, these were categorically proscribed from 1864 on. Individually zemstvos were permitted to take up only routine and technical matters. Any talk of politics and national affairs in zemstvo addresses or petitions was condemned, rejected, on occasion punished.

As a result, it became less and less clear whether the zemstvo was to be a self-governing part of the state structure or a separate government-chartered corporation — or merely a private philanthropic association. Since different ministries, court circles, and ideological currents within the government disagreed and wavered, this question was never settled, and the zemstvo's ambiguous status persisted. As occurs frequently in the life of any bureaucratized autocracy, the zemstvo and its multifarious activities shifted from day to day, subject to the chicaneries or favors — and apathy — of individual officials high and low.

At the outset, the government exercised direct control over the zemstvo by means of a suspensive veto by the local governor and of government approval of most financial decisions — decisions the more important since the zemstvo was expected to support itself by taxing its own constituency. In succeeding years, these original controls over local self-government were repeatedly augmented. The additional restrictions spelled still less autonomy and still less politics:

1866 — Zemstvo taxation of local industry and commerce is limited.

1867 — The jurisdiction of zemstvo assemblies and the contact between individual zemstvos is circumscribed, and the governor's approval is required for publishing zemstvo proceedings.

1869 — Zemstvos are required to put postage on their mails, a minor gesture to emphasize their non-governmental status.

1879 — The main supervisory role over local education is assigned to the marshals of the nobility, with very limited representation for the zemstvos.

1889 — Zemstvo autonomy is considerably reduced by the abandonment of a parallel innovation of the Great Reforms: the previously zemstvo-elected justice of the peace (*mirovoi sudia*) is replaced by a government official (*zemskii nachalnik*), who combines legal with increased administrative jurisdiction over the peasants.

1890 — In the first over-all substitution for the 1864 statute,

1. all members of zemstvo boards become government officials sub-

ject to approval by the governor;
2. the Ministry of the Interior, and the governor as its local representative, are given increased authority to veto zemstvo decisions and to punish board members;
3. the government now appoints the peasantry's delegates to zemstvo assemblies, from lists of candidates submitted by the peasant electors;
4. peasant representation is sharply reduced;
5. only landowners are allowed to be chairmen of zemstvo boards.

This woeful chronology was not accidental. It was bound up with the zemstvo's ambivalent status between self-governing state institution and private philanthropy, with the local friction between zemstvo and government officials, with growing state interference in zemstvo affairs, and — uppermost — with the general belief that the government could crush the zemstvo just as readily, and singlehandedly, as it had originally decreed that institution out of nowhere. All of this encouraged gentry absenteeism and apathy toward the zemstvo, a situation that often left the field to the liberal minority, enabling it to dominate the zemstvo with or without passive peasant support.

The left-right battles in the zemstvo focused on varying issues. In the 1860's the paramount question was most frequently the nature and sources of the zemstvo's self-taxation; in the 1870's it was the zemstvo's role in education; in the 1880's, the size of its budget and hence of its activities. But regardless of the issue, these battles revolved around the same basic zemstvo problems: relation to the government, expansion of activities, aid to the peasantry rather than the landowners.

III

During this gray, unspectacular era, the liberals lacked an organization, an uncensored journal, a clear-cut program, and an identifiable group of theorists or spokesmen. They rightly felt that they were on the defensive, and usually they operated locally and *ad hoc,* truly deserving in this period the appellation "empiricists par excellence."

In the zemstvo Russian liberalism had acquired its foremost "nonpolitical" arena, a substitute for open political activities which the state itself monopolized. After the vastly exaggerated expectations of the Great Reforms era, the liberals cooled toward the zemstvo during the sixties, when its lack of genuine autonomy became unmistakable. Although the liberals had few if any alternatives to the zemstvo, only the late 1870's initiated a new era of liberal enthusiasm. It was less dreamy and intense, more concrete and prosaic than the excitements of the Great Reforms. From then until the 1905 Revolution, liberals directed their enthusiasm and loyalty to the zemstvo as the principal means of furthering their aims.

A unique arena for "nonpolitical" politics had thus been established and recognized as such, and a loose assortment of independently wealthy notables was ready to take advantage of it. But what would they seek to do in the zemstvo and why?

First and last, the liberal notables continued to be noblemen, landowners, gentlemen-farmers or gentlemen of leisure. This did not mean that they could not be rebels or visionaries or activists. But it meant that the gentry notables who embraced the "small deeds" liberalism of this era were themselves people who lived a comfortable, tranquil life — a life in which domestic enjoyments overshadowed cosmic philosophies, a life which they were not tempted to forfeit. These men divided their time between their estates, their residences in Moscow or St. Petersburg, and spas in

Western Europe. Sons of the gentry had begun to study for the professions and to work at them full-time, but in terms of liberal politics this group did not loom large until the end of the century. Rather, the liberal notable usually felt free to abandon himself to the kind of local volunteer activity that Russian society and his own style of life and outlook favored.

Within this rather snug existence, the liberal gentry faced one problem in particular: how to recruit support from below as well as from above. In the middle of the nineteenth century, the most fashionable approach to this problem among Russia's educated minority was provided by populism. This "love of the people" was not confined to the radicals with their agrarian socialism and dreams of peasant revolution. More broadly, populism centered on the belief that Russia's future depended on "the people," the illiterate, drastically backward peasantry — and on raising the material and cultural level of "the people." This task could be accomplished only by the enlightened educated minority. And, under the circumstances, the task must take the form of minute, slow, unspectacular educational and welfare work. Politics, national affairs, reforms must wait.

This nonpolitical *Kulturträger* populism remained a characteristic of the small deeds phase between the 1860's and the 1890's. Its typically Enlightenment reliance on education and humanitarianism, as well as its political motives, were reinforced by economic considerations. For after the agricultural crisis had started in the 1870's, a well-off peasantry became essential for a gentry eager to assure debt repayments and to sell its own land profitably. A complementary economic motive applied in particular to the least agricultural central provinces of European Russia. There a better skilled and more educated peasantry would be likely to squeeze out more income from the barren soil, as well as from the growing handicrafts enterprises and factories.

If the liberal gentry's populism did not call for political action, neither did its other principal approach in the small deeds era. This was the liberals' attempt to win support from above by persuading Russia's illiberal government — in its own terms — that the country, the people, the liberals themselves had earned the reforms the liberals advocated.

In modern times man has tended to regard such unheroic expediency, such prosaic accommodation, with much less favor than he regards wars and revolution, and to condemn it as appeasement. Yet as the nineteenth century grew older, as revolutions throughout Europe boomeranged — either through terror or restoration — against their liberal initiators, and as the status quo took on many liberal features, liberalism in general leaned more and more toward accommodation with the status quo. Like Western liberals, the Russian liberal notables, too, appealed for compromise, gradualism, reasonableness, nonviolence. This mood was not difficult to explain or to defend: politics as such had been proscribed by the state; government dissolution of the zemstvo was a constant threat; an overly oppositional liberalism might lose its backers in the gentry; and, perhaps most important, support from below — whether through spontaneous mass unrest or through the long-range campaign of *Kulturträger* populism — seemed far off. All these stated and unstated considerations explain why small deeds liberalism courted support from above as well as from below. This is why the liberals participated, or even led, when the gentry as a whole and the zemstvo addressed the government in terms of jingo patriotism and monarchist ardor, terms that provoked the satiric comment from Saltykov-Shchedrin's *Fables* which serves as an epigraph for this chapter.[2]

[2] The epigraph: "Although this aspiration to bring his ideals from the empyrean to the field of actuality did smack of something politically dangerous, the Liberal glowed with such sincerity of zeal, and moreover was such a dear and so nice to everyone, that he was forgiven even for

Whether the circumstances and the mood of the period favored *Kulturträger* populism or government accommodation, what was called for was nonpolitical activity, to which nothing was better adapted than local self-government. Restricted to the nonpolitical realm of local education, welfare, and administration, the zemstvo offered unparalleled and officially sanctioned contact with "the people," with the peasant mass of the population. And what better showcase for popular maturity, for national loyalty, and above all for liberal moderation and utility could be devised than a tsar-given, nearly nation-wide institution?

IV

Whereas the gentry concentrated its activities in the zemstvo, the professions developed a variety of additional arenas for their cryptopolitics. Most potent among these were the universities. To be sure, Russian liberalism at the turn of the century was no more dominated by academe than was the "professorial" Frankfurt Parliament of 1848. But the articulateness and public eminence of professors in Russia, as in some other preindustrial societies, placed them in a strategic position. And most liberal currents enabled them to remain within the confines of legal activity, which was important because, as in most continental universities, those in Russia were government financed and government controlled. As Russian liberalism broadened from its gentry base, professors were among the earliest and most prominent adherents from the professions.

The universities substituted in yet another way for proscribed political activities. By expanding tremendously after the middle of the century to accommodate the boom in professional training, they naturally became the first and usually the decisive political stimulant for future members of the professions. In these universities the earliest intelligentsia founded its philosophical circles in the 1830's, and from there populists in the 1870's and Marxists in the 1890's went straight into revolutionary work among the lower classes. Usually, however, student politics meant neither theoretical disputes nor revolutionary agitation, but something between the two. Such political activity most frequently took the form of student disorders: abstention from classes, public rallies, noisy street demonstrations. The immense impact of this species of politics in illiberal societies is still illustrated in Latin America and the Arab world — and more recently in the October Revolution of Poland and Hungary. In Russia it produced a similarly electrifying effect on the still somnolent political life of the 1890's.

The following causes or occasions for student disorders were enumerated at the time by a faculty commission of the University of Moscow:

[1] dissatisfaction with a [university disciplinary] inspector or some professors,
[2] memorial service for a popular writer [1890 and 1891],
[3] memorial service for the victims of the Khodynka misfortune of 1895 [during the Moscow coronation of Nicholas II],
[4] disorders occurring in other universities, as was the case in 1899 [St. Petersburg] and in the current year [1901, Kiev].

Tracing student disorders back to the 1850's, the professors' report noted that since 1887 they had become almost annual at the University of Moscow. This upward trend of student disorders was confirmed by statistics on expulsions from the university, which had doubled in the six years from 1894 to 1899, as compared to the preceding seven years. During the later period, a total of 1214 students were expelled from

being politically unsound. He knew how to vindicate truth with a smile, could, when necessary, play the simpleton, and could show off his disinterestedness to advantage. But chiefly he never demanded anything at the point of the sword, but always only within the limits of possibility."—Saltykov-Shchedrin, *Fables* the University of Moscow; two thirds of them were ousted by the university administration, and almost one third were arrested and exiled by the police.

Whether student disorders were wholly nonpolitical or only externally so, the effect of expulsion was unmistakable. V. K. Plehve — in the 1880's a Deputy Minister of Education and later renowned as the hated pre-1905 Minister of the Interior — plaintively spelled out the consequences:

> For the young people excluded from academic institutions, their lives turn out to be broken up at the very outset. Faced with inactivity, need, and deprivation, they become embittered against the whole social and political order. Those who previously merely leaned toward the seditious teachings now become completely indoctrinated by them. Those who are subjected to administrative exile begin even at the place of exile to exercise a bad influence on the local population. And if upon return they succeed in penetrating once again into institutions of higher learning, they become active agents of secret societies, and their attitude affects their friends. It corrupts them mentally and incites them to all kinds of disorder.

The Deputy Minister of Education goes on to emphasize that student disorders bred the future participants of revolutionary terror. Yet this was not their only consequence. The fact is that these same university perturbations aroused and activated a majority of the professions that embraced liberalism rather than either socialism or revolutionary terror.

A graphic illustration of this comes from the memoirs of Vasili Maklakov, subsequently a leading trial lawyer and the Kadets' golden-tongued orator in the post-1905 Duma. Maklakov's family background had been conservative. Yet in 1887, his freshman year at the University of Moscow, much in Maklakov's life changed when a student struck an unpopular government inspector during a student performance attended by the tsar:

> For the first time in my life I had seen a person who was sacrificing his whole life for something. Involuntarily there passed through my mind my mother's stories about saints who live in this world and what we read about "martyrs" who did not want to renounce their faith. I felt that I was seeing such a "martyr" with my own eyes. This was one of those impressions which in youth do not pass without an impact, although the consequences sometimes varied. This dim emotion possessed not only me apparently. Everyone wanted to do something, to manifest themselves somehow, but did not know what precisely they should do. An age-old tradition helped out.

This age-old tradition was the resort to student disorders. Maklakov became one of Russia's most vocal antirevolutionary liberals, and his first student rally was emphatically apolitical. But it did start him on a career as student spokesman and organizer, of which his later liberal activism was a direct outgrowth.

Again and again in the decade before the 1905 Revolution, at moments when the government was unprepared or unconfident, and the lower classes as usual quiescent, such public manifestations of university students became inflated into national cataclysms. Although student unrests were often locally caused and profoundly nonpolitical, university students identified themselves completely with the professions for which they were heading. Thus they provided the professions, Russia's partial substitute for a business middle class, with an important mass base and striking force all its own. This challenges the commonplace that in modern western history only the concentrated urban lower classes, mainly the factory workers, have the numbers and the hardiness to stand up physically to government force. Nineteenth-century Russia, like other countries today, suggests that university students can rival "the masses." Their youthfulness, their close group contacts, their idealism and intellectuality — all these make university students at times even more effective.

Alongside the universities — and a daily press expanding rapidly since the middle of the century — the professions acquired another arena for their public manifestations. This consisted of a variety of professional and semiprofessional associations. However innocuous their titles or activities might sound, it was in such organizations more than anywhere else that the focal intelligentsia of Moscow and St. Petersburg congregated and interacted during the 1890's. The occasion may have been an anniversary or memorial banquet, a periodic congress, an annual business meeting, a learned lecture, or the report of some obscure subcommission. But no matter what the occasion, the intelligentsia's revival after the oppressive eighties owed much to this new organizational arena in Moscow and St. Petersburg.

Perhaps the most distinguished of these professional associations was the Pirogov Society of Russian Doctors, founded in 1885. Less eminent but more politically oriented was the Moscow Society of Jurisprudence. Established in 1863 as an affiliate of the University of Moscow, it enjoyed considerable autonomy in pursuing its twofold interest in the law and broader political and economic problems. One of its special contributions to the professions was the organization in 1882 of a statistical section, which soon became the center for statisticians and economists throughout the country. Just how successful the Moscow Society of Jurisprudence was as a haven for the intelligentsia may be seen from the fact that in 1899 it was closed on government orders.

A similar fate awaited the oldest learned society in Russia, the Imperial Free Economic Society of St. Petersburg. Founded in 1765 under the sponsorship of Catherine II, it was granted almost complete autonomy — hence the "imperial" and the "free" in the title. In its original purpose it was similar to several dozen agricultural associations throughout the country, including the prominent Imperial Moscow Agricultural Society. All of them were intended to give the landowning nobility assistance on technical and economic questions in agriculture. During the 1890's, however, the Economic Society of St. Petersburg increasingly became a center for the professions rather than for gentleman-farmers. Here professors, agricultural experts, journalists, and leading exponents of feuding socialist camps argued rather freely on current economic issues and government policies. Still more than the Moscow Society of Jurisprudence, the St. Petersburg Economic Society encountered suspicion and increasingly systematic opposition from the government. The climax of this opposition was reached in 1898, when the government insisted on revision of the society's ancient statutes. From 1900 on, the government paralyzed the numerous activities of the society by failing to approve its promptly submitted revisions.

The Moscow Society of Jurisprudence was headed by a leading liberal: Sergei Muromtsev, the first president of the Duma. So was the Economic Society of St. Petersburg, whose president, Count Petr Geiden, belonged to the amorphous middle group in the liberal gentry. Himself a moderate constitutionalist, Geiden by his imposing bearing and skillful diplomacy helped the Economic Society to become the outstanding gathering place for the capital's less moderate intelligentsia. Hence the list of the society's approximately 800 members, and even more so of its officers, reads like a "Who's Who" of the professions' leading liberals and moderate socialists. It is interesting to note that the Moscow Society of Jurisprudence correctly mirrored the predominance in the older capital of the gentry and moderate upper intelligentsia, whereas the Economic Society typified the greater role in St. Petersburg of the professions and of the more radical lower intelligentsia.

Journalists, writers, and literary specialists congregated in a hazy network of St. Petersburg writers' organizations. But hazy as they appeared, these organizations — notably the charitable Literary Fund, founded in 1859 — were quite effective, during moments of public stirring, in channeling the political action of the literati.

Neither so hazy nor so lasting was the last type of organization that served as an arena for the professions: the committees on illiteracy of Moscow and of St. Petersburg. These groups provoked Lenin's jibe because toward the end of the 1880's they began to attract support from the lower intelligentsia (including Lenin's wife-to-be) as a small deeds means of educating "the people." Their network of adult education, of lecture classes, of elementary readings, and grammar textbooks reached into most provinces of Russia. The St. Petersburg Committee on Illiteracy was established in 1861, the year of the Emancipation Act, as a branch of the Economic Society. But its activities lagged until the 1880's when its membership spiraled from 127 to 1025. The Moscow Committee on Illiteracy, a branch of the Imperial Moscow Society of Agriculture, likewise did not come to life until 1890. In both cities, the Committee on Illiteracy was akin to the university as a training ground for future liberal leaders. From the gentry and the professions alike came activists who at the first opportunity exchanged enlightenment for politics.

Given the fact that an autocracy's monopoly forces politically minded elements in the population to adopt substitutes, Russia's new professional middle class was doing rather well in the 1890's. It was not so much their existence itself that made these cryptopolitical and prepolitical arenas of the professions significant. Rather, it was the fact that the traditionalist, bureaucratized Russian monarchy lacked not only the apparatus but also the totalitarian aspirations to keep such organizations completely uncontroversial or loyal. To be sure, the government had its more ravenous officials and its periods of more intensive and more efficient thought control. But during the nineties the government never effectively checked the revival of public life. In this context, between the protracted inertia of the 1880's and the legalized political activity after 1905, the professional and semiprofessional organizations became very important as an invigorating new arena.

V

The only arena for the professions that outweighed these professional associations was the zemstvo, the same network of rural self-government that dominated the public life of the gentry. The zemstvo did not monopolize the professions' activism and devotion as it did the liberal gentry's. The upper intelligentsia remained primarily in numerous courts, in private practice, in university teaching, and in the government. Doctors, teachers, engineers likewise centered their careers as much outside the zemstvo as in it. But for much of the lower intelligentsia, it was the zemstvo that provided the jobs. The growing complexity of agriculture, together with the zemstvo's *Kulturträger* tasks, resulted in an elaborate structure of administrative and technical zemstvo personnel. More and more, this personnel had to be drawn from the professions rather than from either the dilettante gentry or the clerical white-collar workers.

By the 1890's, the zemstvo thus employed thousands upon thousands of doctors, teachers, agronomists, engineers, botanists, veterinarians, economists, and the like. A peculiar importance accrued to the statisticians, whose task was to measure and record land and other property — a staggering and technically crucial task indeed in the Russian countryside, where feudal and traditionalist relationships had prevailed until so recently. The statisticians' special role was further enhanced in 1895, when a government edict placed on the zemstvos themselves the job of evaluating property and levying taxes on it to support their activities.

The zemstvo's professional personnel was universally referred to as "the third element," from a chance remark in 1899, when a Saratov vice-governor ranked it after the government (the zemstvo's first element) and the elective representatives (its second). By that date, this "third element" comprised no less than sixty-five or seventy thousand zemstvo employees. And zemstvo service soon took on a political meaning for these professions as it had for the gentry. The more the other arenas were curbed by government restrictions, the more the zemstvo lured oppositionally inclined members of the professions. To them it became as much a cause, even a way of life, as it was for the liberal gentry. In turn the political orientation, or potential, of the zemstvo was immensely affected by the influx of the intelligentsia. The third element was not rooted in the nobility and was not so firmly linked to rural life and to the zemstvo. The mores and apprehensions that restrained the gentry and even its liberal contingent were largely alien to this lower intelligentsia. Hence in each zemstvo the third element became a democratizing lever exerting a leftward pull.

Nor was the influence of the third element confined to the zemstvo alone. When the government forbade national organizations of third element employees, this group spilled over into the existing professional organizations and soon dominated many of them. Thus within a decade of its founding in the mid-1880's, the Pirogov Society of Russian Doctors was under third element control. Likewise the large and active statistical section of the Moscow Society of Jurisprudence was dominated by this element, as was its successor, the statistical commission of the Economic Society in St. Petersburg. The third element, particularly its activist statisticians, thus provided much of the audience and much of the drive for the professional associations.

One other group felt the impact of the zemstvo third element. This was its employer, the gentry itself. The same factors that resulted in the rise of the professions — the great reforms, industrialization, the country's painful but steady drift away from feudal agriculture — also led to the economic decline of the gentry. A by-product of this decline was the wholesale entry of the younger gentry into the professions, of which by 1900 they made up a sizable minority. It is not surprising that sons of the liberal gentry, having joined the professions, would be particularly active in zemstvo work, either as paid employees in the third element or as landowner delegates in zemstvo assemblies. These professionalized members of the gentry invariably acquired an outlook and even a social status distinct from the class of their origin. Their long and specialized training and their full-time occupations placed them in an impersonal, mobile, and urban atmosphere. This atmosphere was also more demanding and more absorbing than their family's pastoral gentleman-farmer style of life. And yet their whole upbringing, their continuing family ties, often also their continued ownership of land or estates — all this enabled them to influence the gentry as no outside group could.

The outcome was decisive for Russian liberalism. Inside the zemstvo it minimized distinctions between third element and gentry. And it prepared the liberal gentry to follow the intelligentsia leftward.

If we ask, as we did about the gentry, what the professions' ideological trends were, we find two different answers by the 1890's. In the liberal direction, the ideology varied little from that of the liberal gentry, the distinction, if any, lying in the intelligentsia's relatively greater articulateness. For those further left, however, the nineties were a turning point — a period of massive ideological combats and realignments, resulting in a transformation within Russian socialism that affected liberalism profoundly.

Within the professions, the gentry's liberal slavophiles found few echoes. But much of the upper intelligentsia shared the views of the amorphous majority of gentry liberals. Leading jurists and leading professors, particularly, became the spokesmen for Russia's moderate liberals, constitutionalist but antiradical.

* * *

VI

The half-century between the Great Reforms and the 1905 Revolution forms a distinct period in the history of Russian liberalism. More than any other era of Imperial Russia, these decades were marked by industrialization and agricultural crisis. In the zemstvo the Great Reforms had created for liberals a new arena which retained its central role up to the end of the period. During this period, too, the newness, the weakness, and the amorphousness of both liberals and revolutionaries made the relationship between them hazy and politically unimportant. And together the Great Reforms and industrialization spawned the new professional middle class, the "grandsons" of the intelligentsia, which reached political maturity by the turn of the twentieth century.

For a concluding assessment of this period, one may fruitfully compare the Russian varieties of liberal experience. The contrast between the liberalism of the gentry and that of the later intelligentsia appears in their thoroughly different history, temperament, and style of life. The gentry liberals, a small group of financially independent notables, ventured into reformist and philanthropic activities from their often still profitable and leisurely rural existence and the traditional privileges of their class. The intelligentsia, on the other hand, was committed to wholly modern and still novel occupations in a society only half modernizing.

This gulf between styles of life of gentry and intelligentsia explains their different approach to "small deeds" and "senseless dreams," to lesser and tangible improvements as against seemingly more remote and grandiose reforms. Upon its ascendancy in the 1890's and after, the intelligentsia sought actively and without hesitation to replace the gentry's local and mainly cultural small deeds with its own senseless dreams. These were to be national and to aim at nothing less than its twin objectives, constitution and democracy. But as Russian liberalism changed from a cluster of ideals and local activism to an organized national movement, the liberal intelligentsia found itself stymied by a profound tactical problem.

Eager as it was to replace the gentry's small deeds with its own senseless dreams, it continued to need the gentry very badly. Reforms from above, from the *ancien régime,* were the only alternative to revolution — and within a nonrevolutionary, static situation the voice of the gentry had far more impact on officialdom, court, and tsar than that of lower intelligentsia or the masses. Likewise, until the demanded parliament was granted, the vast and gentry-dominated zemstvo structure of rural self-government offered a base of operations preferable to any other in the country. This explains the years of tactical wavering by the otherwise determined intelligentsia majority in the Union of Liberation. It also explains why the intelligentsia continued to conciliate the liberal but nonconstitutionalist and nondemocratic elements of the gentry as it would hardly have done otherwise. . . .

The Liberals After 1905: Revolution or Cooperation with Government?

MICHAEL KARPOVICH

Born and educated in Russia, Michael Karpovich (1888–1959) taught history at Harvard University for over thirty years, exercising a profound influence (both directly and through the work of his students) upon the West's understanding of Russian and Soviet affairs. A man of broad knowledge and catholic intellectual interests, he sought always to achieve the objectivity he considered the mark of the scholar. His writings display a deep faith in liberal principles and democracy, as well as a meticulous avoidance of simplistic explanations of human affairs.

As elsewhere liberalism in Russia was not a homogeneous movement. It proceeded from different social groups, and various motives induced people to join it. This lack of homogeneity was clearly reflected in the make-up of the Constitutional Democratic Party founded in October of 1905. It has been repeatedly pointed out that it came into being as the result of the merging of two forces: the zemstvo liberals, on the one hand, and the liberal-minded part of the professional class, on the other. Strictly speaking, this is an oversimplification. There were other elements in the party which by their social provenience did not belong to either of the two groups, and inside each of the latter there could be found a considerable variety of political attitudes and aspirations. By and large, however, one can accept the accuracy of this summary characterization of the two main components of the Cadet Party, and it is in the light of this division that I am going to discuss the two types of Russian liberalism as exemplified by [Vasilii] Maklakov and [Paul] Miliukov respectively.

* * *

What is of importance is the fundamental cleavage between these two outstanding representatives of Russian liberalism, the difference in the main premises and the general spirit of their political actions. In this case, as in that of many other Russian political trends, the Revolution of 1905 played the part of a catalyst. In Maklakov, it strengthened his fear of all and every revolution, his conviction that revolutionary methods were not only undesirable but in the long run futile. He counted on the evolutionary process in the course of which the regime was bound to change "under the pressure of life itself." In his opinion, it was preferable to try to contribute to the regime's peaceful evolution and not to aim at its complete overthrow. The "historical state power" had one decisive advantage on its side: the people were in the habit of obeying it. It was precisely this inertia of obedience that would be destroyed by a revolution, and with it would go that legal continuity which was so important for the normal growth of a nation. The results could be foreseen on the basis of historical experience: the new government issuing from the revolution either would be so

Reprinted by permission of the publishers from the article by Michael Karpovich, "Two Types of Russian Liberalism: Maklakov and Miliukov," in Ernest J. Simmons (ed.), *Continuity and Change in Russian and Soviet Thought,* Cambridge, Mass.: Harvard University Press, pp. 130–41.

weak that it could not maintain itself in power or else it would be forced to become a ruthless dictatorship.

Maklakov had no illusions as to the nature of the Russian regime of the period. But he still thought that it would be amenable to the pressure of organized public opinion had the liberals used every opportunity to reach an agreement with it, on a program of gradually introduced reforms. In this lay the historical task of Russian liberalism. Maklakov felt that the liberals were missing their chance of contributing to Russia's peaceful evolution by assuming an uncompromisingly hostile attitude toward the regime and thus allying themselves with the destructive revolutionary forces in the country. This appeal to the Acheron (the symbol of the "lower world" in Greek and Latin poetry) was bound to end in the liberals' undoing: their cause would be lost whether revolution won the victory or suffered defeat.

In the eyes of Maklakov the failure of the Russian liberals to approach their political task in a proper spirit became obvious after the proclamation of the constitutional regime. The October Manifesto of 1905 opened a real opportunity for the peaceful solution of Russia's problems, and it was up to the Cadet Party to lead the way in this undertaking. But for this a kind of psychological demobilization was necessary. Unfortunately, the Party could not get rid of its "wartime psychology," and instead of seeking a lasting peace with the government, which could be based on a compromise only, insisted on continuing to wage the struggle until the "final victory. . . ."

Miliukov begins his defense of the Cadet Party by a characteristically empirical reference to the actual conditions in which the Party had to formulate its program and to make its tactical decisions. The Party, he reminds Maklakov, was not living "on abstractions and armchair (*kabinetnye*) deliberations." Its position was shifting now to the right and now to the left, "together with the life of the Russian society." Elsewhere he refers to the psychology of the time — that surge of emotion which was caused by the events of 1905, and from which the rank and file of the Party did not remain immune. He points out that the Party leaders, while trying to maintain the central position, were forced to make occasional concessions to the more impatient spirit of many of their followers. He insists, however, that the Cadet program, while "radical," was not Utopian. What Miliukov means by "radical" becomes clear from his reference to "neoliberalism" as a kindred movement in Western Europe. Back in October 1905, in his opening address at the first ("constituent") convention of the Constitutional Democratic Party, he made the same comparison in slightly different terms: ". . . our Party stands closest to those groups among the Western intellectuals who are known under the name of 'social reformers' . . . our program is undoubtedly the most Leftist of all those advanced by similar political groups in Western Europe."

In a different context, Miliukov accuses Maklakov of stressing the tactics at the expense of the program, attaching more importance to the means than to the aims. He argues that under certain conditions even a liberal might become a revolutionary, and that thus one cannot equate liberalism with a strictly legal way of political action. It is equally erroneous to confuse a defense of the rule of law with that of a given positive law, as Maklakov's reasoning tends to do. Nor should one ascribe such a decisive role to the preservation of legal continuity in the transition from one political order to the other.

If, in these last arguments, Miliukov opposes to Maklakov's traditionalism his own historical relativism, in another case, when dealing with a proper approach to political problems, he blames his opponent for an excessively relativist point of view. Miliukov sees the chief defect of Maklakov the politician in his attempt to transfer into the sphere of politics the psychology and methods of a lawyer. The latter inevitably acquires a professional habit of "seeing a share of truth on the opposite side, and a share of error on his own." A politician cannot allow himself the luxury of such an indifferent and "objective" attitude toward "the contents of truth." Here Miliukov is striking at the very heart of Maklakov's "philosophy of compromise."

Apart from this theoretical disagreement, a radically different interpretation of political events was involved in the controversy. Miliukov did not share in the least Maklakov's optimistic appraisal of Russia's chances of peaceful evolution after the proclamation of the constitutional regime. I have cited above Miliukov's admission that at the time of the publication of the October Manifesto he did not see in it any real change that would induce him to stop fighting the government. Twenty-five years later Miliukov still asserted the correctness of his original diagnosis. Referring to Nicholas II's statement that after the revision of the Fundamental Laws "autocracy remained the same as of old," he declared the Tsar to be closer to the truth than Maklakov, "even from the formal point of view." He also stoutly maintained that the Cadet leaders had been right in repelling the overtures of both Witte and Stolypin, as in neither case had there been any evidence of sincerity. By joining the government on conditions that were proposed to them, Party representatives would have walked into a trap: while being unable to exercise a decisive influence on governmental policies they would have compromised themselves in the eyes of the people. . . .

In the course of time, the difference between Miliukov and Maklakov lost a good deal of its sharpness as far as *tactical* problems were concerned. Events themselves took care of that. By the fall of 1907, the revolutionary energy was totally spent, and there were no visible prospects of its resurgence. The government had recovered its control over the country, and there was a conservative majority in the Duma. The Cadets had to adjust themselves to the new situation. "To preserve the Duma" now became the official slogan. This meant to make the best of the existing circumstances, and to take part in the legislative activity, modest as its scope might be. In this way, the Cadet Party, still led by Miliukov, was moving to the right, in Maklakov's direction. But there was also a reverse process, this time affecting the moderates of the Maklakov type and even those to the right of him. As yet it has not been studied by historians, but it surely can be traced as a slowly but steadily developing trend in the life of the last two Dumas. As the Duma was growing more sure of itself, even its conservative majority was becoming less and less inclined to acquiesce in the arbitrariness of the administration or to overlook its inefficiency. By the end of the period, the opposition spirit in the Duma was by no means limited to the Cadets and those to the left of them. Thus was prepared the ground for the formation of the Progressive Bloc in 1915 and through it for the first Provisional Government.

All this, however, does not deprive the controversy as it developed in 1905–06 of its considerable historical interest. It was then, in a period of crisis, that the two different concepts of an appropriate liberal policy found their fullest and most articulate expression. Essentially, the Russian liberals faced the same problem with which the Social Democrats were struggling at the same time: What was the nature of the transformation Russia was undergoing, and what were its possible limits? Closely linked with this problem was another question: What were the forces in the country that would be able to bring this transformation to a successful conclusion? Maklakov saw the historical need of the hour in the continuation and completion of the Great Reforms of the 1860's, in the establishment in Russia of a political order based on the rule of law and self-government, and he believed that it could and should be effected in an evolutionary way, without the destruction of the existing political and social structure. In his eyes, even a thorough democratization of the latter was not immediately feasible and could be left to the future. For the time being, lasting reforms could be achieved only under the direction of those elements in the country which were prepared for the task by their previous practical experience in the field of public or governmental work. This was why the liberals had to ally themselves with those groups to the right of them which recognized the necessity of reforms, and why they had to seek an agreement with the government whenever an opportunity presented itself. Maklakov minimized the danger of reaction for which he saw no solid base in the prevailing trends of national life. To him, the main danger was on the left and not on the right. It was the danger of uncontrollable and chaotic revolutionary outbreaks, spurred, even if not provoked, by demagogic policies and appeals.

Miliukov expected from the Russian crisis much more far-reaching results than those envisaged by Maklakov. In his concept, the introduction in Russia of a full-fledged parliamentary regime was an immediate necessity and not a program for a more or less remote future. Unlike Maklakov, he considered the country ripe for popular sovereignty, and he felt that it was the duty of the liberals to wage a battle for this aim so long as there was a chance of its attainment. A much more politically minded person than his opponent, he also wanted the constitutional guarantees to be fully spelled out at once. The extreme importance that he attached to institutional arrangements, which to his critics was a sign of his doctrinaire spirit, in reality proceeded from his firm belief in the logic of political institutions. He did not neglect the social aspects of the Russian problem either, and he emphasized the immediate necessity of a radical agrarian reform as vigorously as he fought for political democracy. I know that the Cadet agrarian project, of which Miliukov was one of the sponsors, appeared rather modest as reflected in the peculiarly slanted looking glass of the Russian political life of the time. The fact remains that it proposed compulsory alienation of private property on such a scale as would be deemed revolutionary in any one of the contemporary Western societies. Miliukov knew, of course, that his political and social program could neither win any support among the Russian moderates nor serve as a basis for an agreement with the government. Thus, in pursuing his aims, he was forced to look for allies among the Left-Wing opposition parties, much as he disliked some of their objectives and methods. If Maklakov minimized the danger of reaction, Miliukov at that time apparently minimized the danger of revolution. To him, the real enemies were on the right and not on the left. . . .

THE OFFICIAL–CONSERVATIVES

Pobedonostsev: Preserve the Autocratic System and Its Institutions

ARTHUR E. ADAMS

Arthur E. Adams is Professor of Russian History at Michigan State University. In addition to editing the present work, he is the author of Bolsheviks in the Ukraine *and editor of* Readings in Soviet Foreign Policy *and* The Russian Revolution and Bolshevik Victory. *In the selection presented below the author's intent has been twofold: first, to permit Konstantin Pobedonostsev's writings to explain his political views, and second, to demonstrate how Pobedonostsev persistently, systematically, and with considerable success endeavored to influence the course of Russian political and social affairs after 1881. Among official-conservatives, Pobedonostsev should be classified, along with Tsars Alexander III and Nicholas II, as a* traditionalist, *to distinguish him from such government leaders as Sergei Witte and Peter Stolypin, who were official-conservative* reformers.

KONSTANTIN Petrovich Pobedonostsev, one of Russia's most influential statesmen during the last two decades of the nineteenth century and the first five years of the twentieth, was an outstanding representative of Russian official-conservative thought. His stubborn efforts to preserve the autocracy made him one of the imperial regime's strongest champions and won him the lasting hatred of revolutionary and liberal groups, who likened his character to that of Shakespeare's Iago and referred to him as the "Russian Torquemada," the "Grand Inquisitor of Russia," and the "pace-setter of reaction."

Born in 1827, Pobedonostsev studied law, entered the civil service, and by 1859 had become a professor of civil law at Moscow University. In the early sixties he accepted Tsar Alexander II's invitation to tutor his sons in juridical science. On the death of the heir, Prince Nicholas, in 1865, Pobedonostsev concentrated upon the task of educating the new Crown Prince, Alexander, soon making himself the latter's indispensable advisor. Also in 1865 he became a consulting member of the Ministry of Justice. He had already begun what was to be a lifelong outpouring of essays, translations and monographs, dealing with a variety of legal, political, and moral subjects.

Thereafter the sober and industrious professor of law rose steadily in the government hierarchy. In 1880 he was elevated to the post of Over-Procuror of the Holy Synod — an office which made him the secular head of the Russian Orthodox

From Arthur E. Adams, "Pobedonostsev and the Rule of Firmness," *The Slavonic and East European Review,* XXXII (December 1953), pp. 132–39. By permission of *The Slavonic and East European Review.* The version printed here has been extensively revised.

Church. This post he held until October 1905. Soon after the appointment to the Synod, he received voting membership in the Council of Ministers, a prerogative the Over-Procuror of the Holy Synod had not previously enjoyed. Thus he controlled church affairs and exercised a decisive voice in the highest government councils on all subjects touching upon matters of church and faith. As interpreted by Pobedonostsev for the next twenty-five years, his official position (and his personal relationship with the Tsars) made him responsible for such diverse problems as the appointment of Ministers of State, education, censorship, public morals, the autocracy's defense, and even some aspects of foreign policy.

As a political philosopher, Pobedonostsev is best characterized by the words *caesaro-papist* and *traditionalist*. He based his political thought on the premises that man is by nature *bad* — selfish, lazy, vicious, and uncomprehending — and that mankind's suffering is therefore fundamentally insoluble. Given this essentially hopeless situation he believed that autocracy, based upon the Orthodox faith and the principle of divine right, was the best possible government for Russia. The ruler's primary task was to select Russia's intellectual aristocrats — the few wise, humane, and responsible men each generation provides — as his administrators. He was to set the example for their work by his own high performance, and they in turn would do all that was necessary to balance the conflicting forces within the nation and achieve a peaceful equilibrium in which what was good in man could flourish. The people of the nation, bound in organic union by the Orthodox faith, national tradition and their own inertia, had only to obey and support the absolute ruler.

While in Pobedonostsev's view change and reform were necessary, they were to be carried out with great caution. For the most part the heritage of the past would determine the degree and direction of necessary change; indeed, Russia's historical processes had molded the distinctive characteristics of a political and social system which almost perfectly suited the nation's needs. Despite this guiding role assigned to history, the monarch and his administrators were empowered to violate customs and shatter old institutions when they considered such action necessary, for no lesser tradition or institution could be permitted to limit or compete with the most essential characteristic of Pobedonostsev's model state — the absolute power of the autocrat. Thus the foremost aims of Pobedonostsev's ideal political system were its own self-preservation and defense of the faith and the social institutions supporting it. This political regime was to do its utmost to preserve a stable, quiescent social order and to fight off the demands of foolish rationalists and ignorant fanatics for self-government, improvement of their lot and silly utopias.

In order to implement his political philosophy, Pobedonostsev had to concern himself incessantly with the practical problems of how Russia should be governed. Here his thought was expressed quite simply as a deep conviction that *firmness* was the essential characteristic of good administration. This single quality, he believed, could save Russia if it were systematically manifested by the autocrat and his administrators. Inspired by this conviction he labored tirelessly to make firmness the predominant principle of government, and he grimly opposed the efforts of others to weaken the imperial authority in any way. Because Pobedonostsev's ideas aptly epitomize one type of "official conservatism" and because he personally exerted immense influence on the course of affairs between 1881 and 1905, it is useful to examine more closely, first, the genesis of his concept of firmness, second, the general methods he employed to transform the idea into policy, and third, some of the major battles he fought to give his views predominance.

By his own account Pobedonostsev began to turn against the liberal reforms of Alexander II as early as 1863. In a letter written to the new Tsar, Alexander III, in

1881, he recalled the years after 1862, when he "had seen with deep sorrow how everything was gradually corrupted, how all the principles of honor and duty were destroyed, how weak, indifferent, insignificant people replaced the firm. . . . Together with this," he added, "all our institutions were systematically remade according to false principles. . . . Consequently at the critical moment, not one of these institutions had the strength to serve the state." In 1864 he expressed violent hostility to the reforms in letters to his confidante, Anna Tyutcheva, and again his cry was for firmness and order. To Anna he wrote:

You will not believe how disgusted we are here with the reforms, how we have lost faith in them, how much we should like to stop at something stable, so as to know at last which wheel is really turning and where each worker stands. . . . Really, sometimes a man feels as if he were living among children who imagine they are grown up; judge for yourself how hard this is. And how often, in the whole bazaar of projects, in this noise of cheap and shallow ecstasies, one recalls the words of the psalmist: "The idols of the heathen are but silver and gold, the work of men's hands. They have eyes, but they see not; they have ears, but they hear not. Feet they have, but they walk not; they have mouths, but they speak not. Like unto them are all that trust in them and worship them." In this mart of idols, who is there to rise up and to come in his strength and shatter the idol and proclaim the true God?

There was one man at least "to come in his strength and shatter the idol." In the last years of the reign of Alexander II, Pobedonostsev labored zealously to teach the heir to the throne the "true God" of the autocracy. "And here is what I dare to tell you," he wrote to his pupil in late 1876:

The whole secret of Russian order and prosperity is in the top, in the person of the supreme authority. Do not believe that the subordinates to your authority themselves will limit and regulate things, if you yourself do not limit and regulate. Where you yourself dismiss something, there it is also dismissed by all the land. Your work advances all things, your indulgence and luxury inundate all the land with indulgence and luxury—here is the meaning of that union with the land, to which you were born, and that power which was destined to you from God.

In January 1880 he told the Crown Prince: "The general, growing dissatisfaction arises from the fact that the people do not see unified authority, will and direction, and they lose, little by little, that which is most dear to the people, that is, faith in the government." Then, in the first days of the new Tsar's rule, Pobedonostsev loosed a torrent of notes admonishing his former pupil to stand on the side of firmness. On March 6, five days after the assassination of Alexander II, he wrote to the son: "If they begin to sing the old siren's song, that it is necessary to be calm and to continue in the liberal direction, that it is necessary to yield to so-called public opinion, for God's sake, Your Majesty, do not believe and do not listen! This will be ruin, the ruin of Russia and of you: this is as clear as day to me." Later in the same letter, still arguing to convince the new Tsar, he wrote: "It is necessary to end at once, now, all talk about freedom of the press, about high-handed meetings, about a representative assembly. These are all lies of hollow and flabby people, and it is necessary to reject them for the sake of the *true* people and for the good of the people."

In his efforts to transform his ideas into policy, the self-appointed defender of firmness took full advantage of every weapon that fell to hand. As Over-Procuror he personally intervened to decide matters of faith, to dictate the political opinions of the church hierarchy, and even to select books and pamphlets to be published by the church presses; nor did he hesitate to bend church policy to his own political ends. In addition, as former tutor and trusted friend of Alexander III, he continued to exercise great personal influence over the Tsar, constantly emphasizing the necessity for firmness. Similarly, in the first years of the reign of Nicholas II his influence as Tsarist counselor remained strong, partly because he had tutored Nicholas, partly because he had been councilor to the revered father, partly because in his person were combined the authority of the church and the wisdom of an elder statesman.

By whispering (or thundering) imprecations into the Tsars' ears, Pobedonostsev was able throughout the period of his ascendancy to arrange the appointment and dismissal of many high-ranking officials. The men who owed their appointments to him were subjected to his jealous and constant interference, for he made himself the autocracy's watchdog, attacking ferociously whenever someone he had supported seemed ready to compromise with the forces working toward radical change. His nominees for the post of Minister of the Interior were appointed to that office regularly, from 1881 until 1895. His nominees governed the Ministry of Education from 1881 to 1901, and from 1883 until 1900 he dominated the government's censorship policies through men who served as Chiefs of the Department of Printing Affairs. His influence was continuous and direct during the conservative revision of legal procedures implemented by the Ministry of Justice in the latter half of the 1880's, and a host of lesser officials in many departments came and went as he praised or condemned them in his communications to the Tsars.

By means of his control over both the Synodal and secular presses, Pobedonostsev directed the dissemination of the kinds of literature he thought best suited to Russia's needs. He wrote popular essays and scholarly monographs, translated carefully-selected articles and books from the West, forcefully encouraged conservative journalists and literary men, and just as forcefully suppressed authors whose works he considered dangerous. His was a strenuous and sweeping endeavor to propagandize the nation in favor of the autocracy and the church.

When we turn our attention to Pobedonostsev's defense of his creed and observe him in action, we find that some of the most illuminating evidence is presented by his long struggle against the advocates of liberal reform. He was the sworn enemy of the hope that a body of elected representatives might limit the absolute power of the Tsar. Since this hope for some form of assembly or council with legislative or at least advisory powers was shared by radical and liberal alike in the Russia of 1881–1905, he was compelled repeatedly to launch resolute offensives against the reformers. During his term in office as Procuror of the Holy Synod, he carried out four major campaigns against those who planned the establishment of one or another form of central representative assembly. The first three campaigns he won; the last brought him down; but defeat came twenty-four years after the beginning of his struggle and marked a quarter-century of victory for Pobedonostsev and the conservative forces he represented.

The first trial of strength occurred at the beginning of the reign of Alexander III, in 1881. As is generally known, Alexander II had agreed to the publication of the Loris-Melikov "constitution" on the day of his assassination.[1] A conflict immediately arose between liberal ministers, who wanted the new Tsar to carry out his father's will, and those officials who wanted to quash the projected reform. Pobedonostsev bitterly opposed the "constitution," using all his persuasive powers, in speech and letter, to win the Tsar to his conviction. Torn between rival factions, the young Tsar hesitated; then, persuaded by Pobedonostsev's vigorous rhetoric, he followed the latter's advice, repudiated his other advisers, and rejected reform. The climax of this struggle came at a session of the Council of Ministers on

[1] Count Mikhail Tariyelovich Loris-Melikov, Minister of the Interior. The so-called constitution was actually a plan for the establishment of three preparatory commissions (administrative, financial, and general), composed of appointed experts and supplemented by elected representatives of the *zemstva* and city councils. These commissions were to work with the Council of State in the formation of new laws.

April 29, 1881, when a reactionary manifesto prepared for the Tsar by Pobedonostsev was read:

> In the midst of our great affliction, the voice of God commands us to discharge courageously the affairs of government, trusting in God's providence, with faith in the strength and justice of the autocratic power, which we have been called to support and preserve for the people's good from all impairment and injury. Therefore, let courage animate the troubled and terror-stricken hearts of our faithful subjects, of all lovers of the Fatherland, devoted, from generation to generation, to the hereditary imperial power. Under its shield, and in unbroken alliance with it, our land has more than once lived through great troubles and has grown in strength and glory. Consecrating ourselves to our high service, we call upon all our loyal subjects to serve us and the State in truth and justice in rooting out the horrible seditions that dishonor the land of Russia, in strengthening faith and morality, the good education of the young, the extermination of injustice and plunder, and in the introduction of order and justice in the operation of these institutions presented to Russia by her benefactor, our beloved father.

This manifesto broke the liberals' authority in government and confirmed Pobedonostsev's program. The Minister of the Interior, Loris-Melikov, was defeated; other liberal ministers retired. The Procuror of the Holy Synod had won his first and greatest victory. He followed it up quickly by selecting at the Tsar's request a new Minister of Internal Affairs who could be expected to carry on a government of firmness, Count N. P. Ignat'yev.

The second struggle was to be with this same Count Ignat'yev in 1882, when, without consulting Pobedonostsev, Ignat'yev fostered a plan for a consultative assembly of representatives, which would help his government learn the needs of the country and plan new legislation. Upon learning of the plan and of Ignat'yev's actions to put it into effect, the Over-Procuror acted swiftly to force Ignat'yev out of office. He warned Alexander openly that "if the direction of policy passes to some kind of an assembly, it will mean revolution and the end, not only of government, but of Russia itself"; more deviously, he contrived a scathing denunciation of Ignat'yev's plan in the conservative pages of the quasi-official *Moscow News*. As a consequence of these maneuvers, Ignat'yev was dismissed, and the second trial of strength against the advocates of a representative assembly ended in victory for the champion of firm government.

The third major conflict came in 1895. On the accession of Nicholas II, enlightened and revolutionary circles once again hoped that the time for reform had at last arrived. This hope was shattered by the "Senseless Dreams Speech," delivered by Nicholas to the *zemstvo* representatives assembled at St. Petersburg on January 17, 1895. In this speech Nicholas announced his unswerving adherence to the principle of autocracy in explicit terms:

> I rejoice to see gathered here representatives of all estates of the realm, who have come to give expression to their sentiments of loyal allegiance. I believe in the sincerity of these feelings, which have been those of every Russian from time immemorial. But it has come to my knowledge that lately, at some meetings of the *zemstva,* voices have made themselves heard from people who have allowed themselves to be carried away by *senseless dreams* about the participation of representatives of the *zemstva* in the general administration of the internal affairs of the state. Let it be known to all that I devote all my strength to the good of my people, but that I shall uphold the principle of autocracy as firmly and unflinchingly as did my ever-lamented father.

With the exception of the word "senseless," and a few minor emendations, the address was drafted by Pobedonostsev. It was, in effect, a fresh pronouncement of doom to the Russian liberals and revolutionaries who had dreamed that the new Tsar might lead the way to reform. It aroused intense resentment, which Pobedonostsev was content to characterize as little more than a "sharp muttering in the circles of petty officials and the intelligentsia." He hastened to assure the new Tsar that "now, more than ever, a firm will at the top is necessary in everything. . . ."

Thereafter, having set the new Tsar on the right course, Pobedonostsev labored to keep him moving in the right direction. His influence, however, already weakened during the last years of Alexander III's reign, waned still further under the new Tsar, for Nicholas resented forthright, forceful men, and Alexandra, the Empress, found the spiritual consolation she required among mystical quacks. Nonetheless, Pobedonostsev did not moderate his insistence upon firmness. Four years after the "Senseless Dreams Speech," irritated by the weakness of will he sensed in the Tsar's policies, Pobedonostsev bluntly criticized Nicholas for being frightened of Russian society. "What is our society?" he questioned rhetorically. Here is his answer, offered for the Tsar's enlightenment:

> A mixture of people, belonging to the so-called intelligentsia, extremely variegated, whirling in all directions, a combination of petty officials with an idle crowd of men and women.
>
> Society in Russia was always such. . . . When the government stood and acted on firm principles, then society did not whirl about. Everyone knew thoroughly, without hesitation, what would be permitted by the government and what the government would not suffer in any event. Although the government was silent, everyone knew what it was necessary to expect. . . . Now, this assurance does not exist, and as a result, everything staggers along. [The people of society] . . . have become accustomed to the fact that the government permits everything and is passive, fearing to transgress against some principle written into the law or to disturb some freedom. Even when they make crazy speeches, do crazy things, transgress against order, the government avoids action. . . .

The fourth and final struggle was protracted and painful, and Pobedonostsev gained only limited and temporary victories. Ultimately he was to be defeated by the flood-tides of reform that accompanied the military defeats of the Russo-Japanese War and the Revolution of 1905. The first phase of this struggle occurred in 1904, when Prince Svyatopolk-Mirsky brought forward a plan to enlarge the State Council with representatives elected by important public institutions. This project, Pobedonostsev and Count Sergei Witte successfully blocked. The next phase came to light when the official gazette, on February 18, 1905, published two contradictory state documents (a manifesto and an ukase). The manifesto began as follows:

> Ill-intentioned leaders of these insurrections, blinded by arrogance, are daring to attack the foundations of the Russian Empire, sanctified by the Orthodox Church and supported by law. They are seeking to break the chain that connects Us with Our past, to disrupt the existing state structure, and to establish in its place another form of government, foreign to Our country. . . . Let all Russians stand firm around Our Throne, true to the traditions of Our past . . . and support the autocracy for the good of all Our faithful subjects.

The ukase to the Senate ordered the Council of Ministers to "examine and consider the ideas and suggestions presented to Us by private persons and institutions concerning improvements in the state organization and the betterment of the people's existence." Thus the manifesto restated the autocracy's determination to stand firm, while the ukase hinted that some form of representation was being considered.

Pobedonostsev's hand appears in the manifesto. Although he had enthusiastically approved of an early draft submitted to him by Nicholas, he had at the same time suggested minor changes, reiterating the necessity of preserving the Tsar's authority. The final text embodied his suggestions. Despite this desperate, last-minute effort to preserve the autocracy, the manifesto fell by the roadside. The ukase, expressing, as it did, what was then an almost universal desire for representation in government, became the center of popular and official interest.

Pobedonostsev, however, was not yet ready to withdraw from the struggle. During the summer of 1905 the ukase was to be elaborated into a new manifesto establishing a State Duma. On July 30 it was Pobedonostsev himself, the sworn enemy of the representative assembly, who was chosen by Nicholas II as president of the special committee responsible for the manifesto establishing such an assembly. When, on August 6, 1905, this new manifesto was published, together with a decree for the establishment of the State Duma, it was not surprising that the projected assembly was exclusively consultative. In the very act of appearing to grant the long-awaited reform, Pobedonostsev's drafting committee had managed to preserve the autocracy. Clearly, as late as August 1905, Pobedonostsev played an important role in the suppression of representative government in Russia. At this late date, he could still believe that he had been right when he had written in his *Moskovskiy Sbornik:* "Providence has preserved our Russia, with its heterogeneous racial composition, from the misfortunes . . . [attendant upon a multitional parliament]. It is terrible to think of our condition if destiny had sent us the fatal gift — an all-Russian parliament! But that will never be!"

He had never been more mistaken. Two months after Pobedonostsev's August success, the swift surge of revolution compelled Nicholas to sign Count Witte's Manifesto of October 17, which gave the State Duma immensely expanded powers. Pobedonostsev was swept out of office, his personal influence ended, his very name cursed by those enemies who troubled to remember it. Yet though the defeat was absolute, it must be recognized that for a grim twenty-four years he had been the victor. Along with other men who shared his convictions, he had held the dyke of firm government against the revolutionary flood until the cause of firmness was swept aside. And even as he retired from the scene, the faith which he had propagated for so many years — a firm autocracy as the sole good government — remained strong in the minds and hearts of many influential Russians.

Save Russia by Rapid and Forceful Industrialization

SERGEI WITTE

Brilliant and arrogant, Count Witte was Russia's Minister of Finance from 1892 until 1903. Striving to preserve the autocracy by instituting economic reforms that would make the nation strong, Witte encouraged the influx of foreign capital, maintained high protective tariffs, and supported industrialists with government loans and subsidies. His forceful economic policies immensely increased railroad building in the 1890's, stimulating a widespread growth of industry. Like Pobedonostsev, Witte believed absolutism to be the highest form of government, a belief based upon the assumption that the autocrat would always be wise and responsible. But Nicholas II was neither, and in the "Secret Memorandum" to the Tsar, written in 1899 and reprinted in part here, the Minister of Finance tried to explain the principles of his economic policy and pleaded for the Tsar's firm support.

REPORT OF THE MINISTER OF FINANCE TO HIS MAJESTY ON THE NECESSITY OF FORMULATING AND THEREAFTER STEADFASTLY ADHERING TO A DEFINITE PROGRAM OF A COMMERCIAL AND INDUSTRIAL POLICY OF THE EMPIRE. EXTREMELY SECRET

The measures taken by the government for the promotion of national trade and industry have at present a far deeper and broader significance than they had at any time before. Indeed, the entire economic structure of the empire has been transformed in the course of the second half of the current century, so that now the market and its price structure represent the collective interest of all private enterprises which constitute our national economy.

As a result of such fundamental transformation of the economic interests of the country, every major measure of the government more or less affects the life of the entire economic organism. The solicitude shown to various branches of industry, a new railroad, the discovery of a new field for Russian enterprise, these and other measures, even if partial and of local application only, touch the entire ever more complicated network and upset the established equilibrium. Every measure of the government in regard to trade and industry now affects almost the entire economic organism and influences the course of its further development.

In view of these facts, the minister of finance concludes that the country, which in one way or the other is nurtured by the commercial and industrial policy of the government, requires above all that this policy be carried out according to a definite plan, with strict system and continuity. Isolated and unco-ordinated acts of encouragement can never offset the pernicious and painful shocks which the economic organism suffers from a change of the guiding policy. Even the most beneficial measures of the government in the realm of economic policy during the first years of their operation often seem to impose a hardship on the population. It is a difficult matter; years, even decades, must pass before the sacrifices can bear fruit. Wise statesmanship requires, then, that these difficult years be suffered patiently, as the experience of other peoples shows that the sacrifices demanded by the coherent and steadfast adherence to a firm

From Theodore H. Von Laue, "A Secret Memorandum of Sergei Witte on the Industrialization of Imperial Russia," *The Journal of Modern History,* XXVI (March 1954), 60–74. By permission of Theodore von Laue and *The Journal of Modern History*. In the original article Von Laue's translation of the "Secret Memorandum" is accompanied by an excellent introduction.

and just economic system are always rewarded a hundred fold. Any change of basic policy before the fruits of sacrifice have had time to mature leads to the complete loss of all capital invested in the previous system, or it leads to new sacrifices in the pursuit of a new system. A government with an unsteady commercial and industrial policy is like a businessman who constantly reorganizes his production without producing anything. No matter how great the technical perfection of such a business, it always ends in ruin.

When I became minister of finance, I acted on the conviction that the government, no matter which commercial and industrial system it follows, is guided by the property interests of the entire people and that in order to compensate them for their losses one has merely to wait for the positive results of the government's economic system. This lasts years and sometimes decades. In taking over the ministry of finance in 1892, I felt obliged to make clear to myself the foundations of the commercial and industrial policy of my predecessors and to bend all efforts toward continuing and finishing what they had begun or had taken over from their predecessors. The necessity of such succession and continuity seemed to me so paramount that I relinquished my own personal views. I realized, of course, that there were very weighty arguments against the protectionist system and against high tariffs. But I supposed that even the proponents of free trade must be aware that it would be extremely harmful from the government view point to repudiate the protective system before those industries had been securely established for whose creation whole generations had paid by a high tariff. I assumed that an absolutely perfect tariff system did not exist and that each system had positive and negative features. And I furthermore concluded that in making a choice one should throw one's weight in favor of the system already existing, for which the people bore such heavy sacrifices and to which the country's economy is already adapted. Besides, it was clear to me that any commercial and industrial policy touching very directly the property interests of the population would always have its defenders and opponents. I considered it my duty to listen attentively to the latter, and I recognized the necessity of alleviating the measures which inevitably brought temporary damage to some. Nevertheless, I did not waver in my fundamental aim to complete in detail what was so boldly begun in the reign of Alexander III and of Your Imperial Highness. The results of state policy in economic matters are the work of decades, and the most harmful of all commercial and industrial systems is that which is inconstant and wavering.

These conclusions find special confirmation in the facts of our industrial development. The absence of a strictly enforced plan and sudden changes from protectionism to almost unlimited free trade did not permit our industry to develop calmly. What was created yesterday was destroyed today; and only by the will of Emperor Alexander III was a customs tariff established which gave positive protection to our industries. His wise command was realized in the tariff of 1891, which was worked out while I was still one of the directors of the departments in the ministry of finance. It has been the starting point of our industrial system.

Now, as the attacks on the existing commercial and industrial policy continue and even increase in bitterness, I consider it my duty to review once more its chief foundations and to submit them to Your Imperial Highness. In order to be the true executor of Your Imperial Majesty's will, I must have instruction not for individual measures but for a comprehensive commercial and industrial policy. The country needs, above all, a firm and strict economic system.

In Russia at the present moment the protectionist system is in force. Its principal foundations were laid down in the tariff of 1891.

What are the tasks of the protectionist system?

Russia remains even at the present essentially an agricultural country. It pays for all its obligations to foreigners by exporting raw materials, chiefly of an agricultural nature, principally grain. It meets its demand for finished goods by imports from abroad. The economic relations of Russia with western Europe are fully comparable to the relations of colonial countries with their metropolises. The latter consider their colonies as advantageous markets in which they can freely sell the products of their labor and of their industry and from which they can draw with a powerful hand the raw materials necessary for them. This is the basis of the economic power of the governments of western Europe, and chiefly for that end do they guard their existing colonies or acquire new ones. Russia was, and to a considerable extent still is, such a hospitable colony for all industrially developed states, generously providing them with the cheap products of her soil and buying dearly the products of their labor. But there is a radical difference between Russia and a colony: Russia is an independent and strong power. She has the right and the strength not to want to be the eternal handmaiden of states which are more developed economically. She should know the price of her raw materials and of the natural riches hidden in the womb of her abundant territories, and she is conscious of the great, not yet fully displayed, capacity for work among her people. She is proud of her great might, by which she jealously guards not only the political but also the economic independence of her empire. She wants to be a metropolis herself. On the basis of the people's labor, liberated from the bonds of serfdom, there began to grow our own national economy, which bids fair to become a reliable counterweight to the domination of foreign industry.

The creation of our own national industry — that is the profound task, both economic and political, from which our protectionist system arises. The advantages derived from the successful completion of this system are so numerous that I select here only the principal ones.

National labor, which at present is intensively employed only for a short agricultural season, will find full application and consequently become more productive. That, in turn, will increase the wages of the entire working population; and that again will cause an improvement of the physical and spiritual energy of the people. The welfare of Your Empire is based on national labor. The increase of its productivity and the discovery of new fields for Russian enterprise will always serve as the most reliable way for making the entire nation more prosperous.

The demand not only for raw materials but also for other articles will be met to a considerable extent by the work of the people themselves. And consequently the payment to foreigners, which at present consumes a considerable part of our national revenue, will be reduced. The import of foreign goods will then be determined not by the weakness of our industry but by the natural division of labor between nations, by which an industrially developed nation buys abroad only what it cannot advantageously produce at home; purchase abroad then enriches rather than exhausts it. Thanks to that, the accumulation of new capital from national savings is considerably facilitated, and that, in turn, promotes a further growth of productivity.

Within the country, exchange between the products of the soil and of labor will expand and give greater purchasing power to the grain market, which then can afford to pay higher prices for agricultural goods, thanks to which export prices also will rise. As a result, the income derived from land will also increase. And that, in turn, will make it possible for land cultivators, small and large, to improve their agricultural techniques and to raise the productivity of the land. The improvement of agricultural techniques will inevitably reduce the extreme fluctuation of harvests, which at present imposes such a heavy strain upon our national prosperity.

The gradual growth of industry in the country, always accompanied by falling prices for manufactured goods, will make it possible for our export trade to deal not only in raw materials, as at present, but also in industrial goods. Our present losses in the European trade can then be converted into profits in the Asiatic trade.

Popular welfare and state finance will find firm support not only in agriculture but also in industry and will gain considerably greater steadfastness and strength thereby.

Such are the great tasks of the protectionist system, which was steadily applied to Russia, beginning with the reign of Alexander III. But a great task also demands heavy sacrifices. . . .

Of all charges against the economic policy of Russia, the minister of finance is most keenly aware of the following: that because of the tariff a Russian subject pays for many items considerably more than the subjects of other countries; that the costs of production rise in proportion as they are determined by the value of capital goods; that the cost of living also grows for both rich and poor; and that the paying powers of the population are strained to the utmost, so that in many cases consumption is directly curtailed. The minister of finance recognizes that the customs duties fall as a particularly heavy burden upon the impoverished landowners and peasants, particularly in a year of crop failure. These imposts are a heavy sacrifice made by the entire population, and not from surplus but out of current necessities. Naturally, the question is asked: Are there no ways to avoid or to reduce those sacrifices which have such an enervating effect on our economy?

It must be stated first of all that the system, because it is coherently carried out, is already beginning to show results. Industry numbers now more than 30,000 factories and mills, with an annual production surpassing 2,000,000,000 rubles. That by itself is a big figure. A widespread and tight net of economic interests is linked to the welfare of that industry. To upset it by a shift to free trade would undermine one of the most reliable foundations of our national well-being; such a shock would adversely affect its general level. In several branches, our industry grew very rapidly. Thus the smelting of pig iron, not exceeding 10,000,000 pood at the beginning of the century, rose to 36,000,000 pood in the last decade and to 114,000,000 pood in 1897, i.e., it trebled in ten years. And if it did not meet the demand, it was only because the demand itself rose from 102,000,000 pood in 1893 to 166,000,000 pood at present. In 1893, 131,000,000 pood were smelted. Still more characteristic was the development of the cotton industry, which produces goods of wide popular consumption. That industry formerly used foreign raw materials exclusively; at the present, thanks to the protective tariff, it obtains up to 30 per cent of the required cotton inside the empire. Its annual productivity grew from 259,000,000 rubles in 1885 to 531,000,000 rubles in 1896, i.e., more than double. The import of yarn from abroad fell from 296,000 pood to 127,000 pood. Now the value of imported cotton fabrics does not exceed 5,000,000 rubles, and that is accompanied by a noticeable increase of exports from Russia to Persia, Bokhara, Middle Asia, China, etc. That export, which amounted to 3,500,000 rubles in the past decade, now attains 12,000,000 rubles.

In this way the sacrifices of the population are not borne in vain. Industry has grown very considerably as compared with the condition in which the tariff of 1891 found it. Russian enterprise has found itself new outlets; internal trade has developed. But much remains still to be done before we can say that the building is finished. . . .

It is obvious that our domestic industry, no matter how extensively it has developed, is quantitatively still small. It has not yet reached such proportions as to give birth to the creative forces of knowledge, the mobility of capital, and the spirit of enterprise. It has not yet attained the pitch of healthy competition which would enable it to produce cheaply and repay the population for its sacrifices by the cheapness and abundance of its products. It is not yet an equal partner of agriculture in providing goods for export and bearing the tax burden. But that partnership must be accomplished, and in the shortest time possible. Economic conditions in the past years have become very complex, and the protective tariff has borne down extremely heavily upon the population. It has been too difficult for the population to provide for both itself and an almost monopolistic industry. The task of our present commercial and industrial policy thus is still a very difficult one. It is necessary not only to create industries but to force them to work cheaply; it is necessary to develop in our growing industrial community an energetic and active life — in a word, to raise our industries qualitatively and quantitatively to such a high level that they cease to be a drain and become a source of prosperity in our national economy.

What do we need to accomplish that? We need capital, knowledge, and the spirit of enterprise. Only these three factors can speed up the creation of a fully independent national industry. But, unfortunately, not all these forces can be artificially implanted. They are mutually interconnected; their own proper development depends upon the very growth of industry.

The accumulation of capital is possible only to the extent that the productivity of an enterprise yields an unused surplus. In Russia, where the great majority of the population is still engaged in agriculture, that surplus of income over expenditure is insufficient for the accumulation of new capital. Actually, the savings of which account is kept — those which go into banks and savings institutions — amount to about 200,000,000 rubles a year. And a considerable part of them (about 130,000,000 rubles) is spent for the purchase of mortgages from land banks, i.e., they are consumed by the needs of rural and urban economy. The creation of larger funds — say, for the construction of railways — always requires the help of the government in our country. Only the industrial regions of Your Empire show a real ability to create new capital for economic application. This capital appears also as the chief promoter of our industrial progress. But, as the influence of these industrial regions in our vast national economy is relatively small, these savings seem insufficient for the quick creation of an independent national industry.

We have thus neither capital, nor knowledge, nor the spirit of enterprise. The extension of popular education through general, technical, and commercial schools can have, of course, a beneficial influence; and Your Majesty's government is working on that. But no matter how significant the promotion of enlightenment, that road is too slow; by itself, it cannot realize our goal. The natural school of industry is first of all a lively industry. Institutions of learning serve only as one aid toward that end. The first investment of savings awakens in man the restlessness of enterprise, and with the first investment in industry the powerful stimulus of personal interest calls forth such curiosity and love of learning as to make an illiterate peasant into a railway builder, a bold and progressive organizer of industry, and a versatile financier.

Industry gives birth to capital; capital gives rise to enterprise and love of learning; and knowledge, enterprise, and capital combined create new industries. Such is the eternal cycle of economic life, and by the succession of such turns our national economy moves ahead in the process of its natural growth. In Russia this growth is yet too slow, because there is yet too little industry, capital, and spirit of enterprise. But we cannot be content with the continuation of such slow growth. No matter how great the results attained by the present protectionist system, to accomplish what is still ahead and what the entire country so impatiently waits for is by all accounts the most difficult matter. We have to develop mass-production industries, widely dispersed and variegated, in which not customs duties but the more powerful and beneficial laws of competition play the dominant role.

We must give the country such industrial perfection as has been reached by the United States of America, which firmly bases its prosperity on two pillars — agriculture and industry. In order to reach these ultimate goals, we must still pass through the most difficult stretch of the road we have chosen. We have not only to direct the flow of capital into this or that field or to find new spheres for its investment, but we have to have above all a great abundance of capital, so that by its natural competition it undermines its own present monopoly position. But not even the most powerful government can create capital.

What, then, must we do?

We cannot wait for the natural accumulation of capital in a country in which the majority of the population is experiencing hard times and which surrenders a considerable part of its surplus to the government in the form of taxes. And we cannot continue to make the population pay dearly for what it buys — that is too much of a burden for the population and for agriculture, its primary occupation. Neither can we repudiate the protectionist system and grant free or at least easier access to foreign goods; we cannot thus give up the industries which the people created with such heavy sacrifices — for that would mean to deprive the country, already so destitute of capital, of the industries which it has protected by the sweat of its brow.

This dilemma would be fatal to our economy, if the government, powerless to create new capital in sufficient quantity, were not in a position to hasten the influx of capital into the empire from states which have a surplus of it.

The influx of foreign capital is, in the considered opinion of the minister of finance, the sole means by which our industry can speedily furnish our country with abundant and cheap goods. Each new wave of capital, swept in from abroad, knocks down the immoderately high level of profits to which our monopolistic entrepreneurs are accustomed and forces them to seek compensation in technical improvements, which, in turn, will lead to price reductions. Replenishing the poor store of popular savings by foreign capital makes it possible for all capital in the country to flow more freely over a broader field and to work up not only the fat but also the leaner sources of profit. Hence the natural riches of the Russian land and the productive energies of its population will be utilized to a considerably greater extent; our economy will begin to work with greater intensity. It will be difficult to say then whether foreign capital or our own productive forces, invigorated and given a chance by foreign capital, will have the greater influence over the further growth of our industries.

But in recent times objections have been raised against the influx of foreign capital. It is said that this influx is detrimental to basic national interests, that it tries to siphon off all profits from our growing Russian industries, that it will lead to the sale of our rich productive forces to foreigners. It is no secret, of course, to the minister of finance that the influx of foreign capital is disadvantageous primarily to entrepreneurs, who are harmed by any kind of competition. Not only our own, but also foreign, capitalists who have already obtained an advantageous place in Russian industry join in these heart-rending complaints and thus try to guard their monopolistic profits. But, as frequently happens in the public discussion of economic problems, the interested voices are hiding behind impartial but little-informed representatives of public interests; and what is undesirable for private groups is, by a misunderstanding, eagerly interpreted as harmful to our economy as a whole.

The extent of the influx of foreign capital into Russia is usually much exaggerated. The foreign corporations formed in 1896 numbered twenty-two, with a basic capital of 80,000,000 rubles. In 1897 their number was fifteen, with 55,000,000 rubles capital. Even if one adds foreign capital invested in Russian corporations (12,000,000 rubles in 1896 and 22,000,000 in 1897) one finds that, all together, foreign capital does not amount to more than one-third of the capital of all joint-stock companies formed annually. One should also remember that the corporation is still something very strange and unpopular with Russian entrepreneurs. The organization which they prefer is the personal enterprise or at least the family partnership. A considerable part of Russian capital is invested in such enterprises; the number of these formed every year equals that of the joint-stock companies. It would seem, then, that of the total amount of capital invested every year in the further development of our industries, foreign capital scarcely constitutes more than one-fifth or one-sixth.

Ninety-two million rubles in 1896; 77,000,000 rubles in 1897; 376,000,000 rubles all together since 1887 — do these statistics prove that there is a danger for our vast Russian economy? Can our productive forces be sold at such a figure? That much foreign capital is no more than a leaven, which derives its significance not from its size but from the energy which it sets free in our sluggish industrial community. Foreign capital, five times smaller than Russian, is nonetheless more visible; it arouses attention because it carries with it better knowledge, more experience, and more initiative. But it deposits these cultural forces in Russia, and with that we really cannot find fault.

There are complaints that our protectionist system obstructs the import trade, that we do not bring in many foreign goods but instead open our doors wide to foreign capital. As a matter of fact, we imported foreign capital to the amount of 92,000,000 rubles in 1896 and 77,000,000 rubles in 1897, but foreign goods to the amount of 585,000,000 rubles and 560,000,000 rubles, respectively, i.e., six or seven times more than capital. But, on the other hand, if we look more deeply into the character of foreign capital, we find that in the last analysis it flows to us not in the form of money — our currency is furnished with a sufficient quantity of tokens — but, by a complex exchange process, in the form of useful goods. The import of foreign capital constitutes a part of the import of foreign goods, but with the difference that it is not spent for immediate consumption by the population but saved for productive purposes, for constructive investment in industry.

If we compare our import from abroad for the past years (1896 and 1897) with the average for the years 1888–90, we see that the import of pig iron, iron ore, steel, machines, apparatus, iron and steel products, iron ships — in a word, of capital goods which have long been protected and are necessary not for the consumer but for the producer — amounted to 98,000,000 rubles in 1896 (when 92,000,000 rubles of foreign capital was imported). In 1897 it amounted to 82,000,000 rubles (when 77,000,000 rubles of foreign capital was imported). In the woolen and silk industries the import of thread fell off and was replaced by the import of raw wool and silk, as the processing of these raw materials for the domestic consumer was done more and more by our own industries. In the cotton industry the import of finished goods, thread, and even raw cotton declined. It is obvious that the very character of our import changes; consumers' goods are replaced by producers' goods. And it seems hardly understandable to the minister of finance when it is said in the same breath that it is advantageous for the country to buy abroad, say, cotton fabrics year after year and yet that it is harmful for the same country to buy abroad the machines which could produce such fabrics inside the country. Why does everybody wholeheartedly approve if a country does not consume all its income but spends part of it for further production, and why should they at the same time consider it a danger if it practices equal thrift with its foreign purchases?

Apparently such falsehoods grow from dissatisfaction with the fact that the revenue from these new enterprises will go to the foreign capitalists and that the owners of the imported machinery which is set to work in the country will also be foreigners.

But then the factories which produce abroad for the Russian consumer also belong to foreigners and are also founded by foreign capital; their revenue does not go to Russia, either. But there is a basic difference: the machinery imported into Russia and set to work here, even though it belongs to a foreigner, operates in a Russian setting. And it will not work by itself. It demands raw materials, fuel, lighting, and their auxiliary materials, and it demands human labor. All that, its owner must buy in Russia. Taking all this into account, it seems that the greater part of a ruble spent for any product of foreign enterprise at work on Russian territory goes for the payment of various ingredients of production bought inside the country; and only the remaining part goes to the foreign capitalist as reward for his capital, knowledge, enterprise, and risk. How much of the price of a given commodity goes to the worker and how much to the entrepreneur may be seen, for instance, from analyses published by the American department of labor about the relationship between wages, entrepreneurial profit, and the price of goods. In the cotton industry 30 per cent goes to the workers, but only 6½ per cent to the entrepreneur; in the glass industry 38 per cent goes to the workers, but only 9 per cent to the entrepreneur; in metallurgy and machine-building, 35 per cent to the worker and 10 per cent to the entrepreneur; in railway companies, 34 per cent to the workers and less than 3 per cent to the entrepreneurs. In this manner, out of one ruble paid for the finished commodity produced with the help of foreign capital, approximately 25–40 kopecks accrue to the Russian worker. Another considerable part is spent for raw materials and other auxiliary items, and only 3–10 kopecks is left as the entrepreneur's profit. But in paying for an imported commodity, the entire ruble leaves the country; and neither the producers of raw materials and fuel nor the worker receives a single kopeck. The complaint about the exodus of part of the income as reward for the application of foreign capital would have full weight only if we had a choice between Russian capital and foreign capital and only if we could hope that the former could fulfil not only its own present function but also that now performed by foreign capital. As that is not the case, one has to compare the merits of the following two propositions. Which is better, to import finished goods or to draw from abroad foreign capital, which enables our Russian productive forces to manufacture them here at home? Either way we have to pay the foreigner, but obviously in the case of imported capital that payment will be considerably less than in the case of imported goods.

One has to consider also the fact that it is generally held advantageous to sell finished goods and dangerous to sell productive forces. The buyer obviously must be guided by the contrary principle. If in our present situation we cannot satisfy all our demands from our own resources and have to resort to purchasing abroad, it will be more advantageous for us to buy not finished goods but capital, which is one of the most necessary productive forces, particularly in industry. This consideration apparently is lost sight of by those who look so apprehensively at the prospect of paying dividends to foreigners. . . .

Considering the fact that the influx of foreign capital is the chief means for Russia in her present economic condition to speed up the accumulation of native capital, one should . . . wish that our legislation concerning foreigners might be simplified. Historical experience shows that those human energies which accompany foreign capital are a useful creative ferment in the mass of the population of the most powerful nation and that they become gradually assimilated: mere economic ties change into organic ones. The imported cultural forces thus become an inseparable part of the country itself. Only a disintegrating nation has to fear foreign enslavement. Russia, however, is not China!

I have now analyzed the chief bases of the economic system which has been followed in Russia since the reign of Alexander III.

Its starting point is the protective tariff of 1891, somewhat lowered by the subsequent trade treaties with France, Germany, Austria-Hungary, and other governments.

That protective system has for its aim the creation of a Russian national industry, which would contribute to the growth of our economic, and consequently also our political, independence and would make possible more favorable terms for both international and domestic trade.

That task, demanding great sacrifices from the population, has in some respects already been fulfilled. Russia has now an industry of tremendous size. The interests of our entire economy are closely tied to its future.

This industry, however, has not yet reached such an extent and such technical perfection as to furnish the country with an abundance of cheap goods. Its services cost the country too dearly, and these excessive costs have a destructive influence over the welfare of the population, particularly in agriculture. They cannot be sustained much longer.

We cannot possibly count on an adequate growth of our industry out of our own national resources, because our store of capital, knowledge, and the spirit of enterprise is altogether insufficient to provide us with cheap industrial goods.

To obtain cheaper goods, of which the population stands in such urgent need, by a substantial tariff reduction would be too expensive. It would forever deprive the country of the positive results of the protective system, for which a whole generation has made sacrifices; it would upset the industries which we have created with so much effort just when they were ready to repay the nation for its sacrifices.

It would be very dangerous to rely on the competition of foreign goods for the lowering of our prices. But we can attain the same results with the help of the competition of foreign capital, which, by coming into Russia, will help Russian enterprise to promote native industry and speed up the accumulation of native capital. Any obstructions to the influx of foreign capital will only delay the establishment of a mature and all-powerful industry. The country cannot afford to defer that goal for long. The burden of expensive manufactured goods so oppresses the population that, unless we resort to the help of foreign capital for the quick development of our industry, it would be better to give up the tariff of 1891 altogether. Without the help of foreign capital, which can create an industry in a country surrounded by high tariff barriers, a tariff is merely preventive and not creative; such a tariff can destroy a country. The tariff of 1891 was a beneficial measure only because of the subsequent trade treaties and of the influx of foreign capital. One cannot give up these logical corollaries and not run the risk of rendering the original measure harmful to national welfare.

As our industries grow with the help of foreign capital, it will be possible gradually and in strict accordance with the course of our industrial development to lower our tariffs. Such reduction, however, ought to be timed to the renewal of our trade treaties, because, without a cautious reduction adjusted to the conditions of our industry, we will not be able to defend the interests of our foreign trade. The coming renewal of our trade treaties on favorable terms will be a difficult matter economically as well as politically. In dealing with countries which buy our agricultural exports, we should insist on their lowering their tariffs for our goods. But this time the conflict with the interests of native agriculture in these countries with whom we must deal may be even more bitter than at the time of the memorable tariff war with Germany. It will be possible to obtain from them better conditions for our exports only if we, on our part, are in a position to offer them lowered tariffs for their industries. A trade agreement is nothing but a mutual exchange of such tariff reductions. If we voluntarily reduce our tariff before 1904 without receiving compensation from foreign governments, then we cannot induce them to reciprocate at the time of the conclusion of a new treaty. They not only will not agree to making concessions to our exports but under pressure from their native agrarians might even raise their barriers. That is the reason why our protective tariff should stand unchanged until 1904.

If we carry our commercial and industrial system, begun in the reign of Alexander III, consistently to the end, then Russia will at last come of age economically. Then her prosperity, her trade and finance, will be based on two reliable pillars, agriculture and industry; and the relations between them, profitable to both, will be the chief motive power in our economy. Russia will move closer to that goal with the help of foreign capital, which, anyway, is required to make the protective tariff of 1891 effective.

Your Imperial Highness may see from the foregoing that the economic policy which the Russian government has followed for the last eight years is a carefully planned system, in which all parts are inseparably interconnected. Other persons, perhaps, can devise a better system to establish the needed equilibrium more successfully in a different way. Upon assuming the direction of the ministry of finance, I found a protective system almost in full operation. This system seemed to me then, and still seems to me now, completely justified. I bent all my efforts to speed its beneficial results and to alleviate, principally with the help of foreign capital, the hardships of the transition period. It is possible that we could have pursued a different policy. But in following the directives of Your Imperial Highness in such an intimately interdependent matter as our national economy, I believed it my duty as minister of finance to ask Your Majesty to consider this point: even if it were possible to follow a different economic policy, it would, no matter how beneficial its ultimate results, produce in the immediate future a sharp break. Such an unnecessary shock would aggravate the hardships now existing. Only by a system strictly sustained, and not by isolated measures, can a healthy development be guaranteed to our national economy.

Pledging all my efforts to fulfil still better the will of my sovereign, I make bold to ask that it may please Your Imperial Highness to lend your firm support to the foundations of our economic system as I have analyzed them. They form, in essence, the following program:

1. To keep the tariff of 1891 unchanged until the renewal of our trade treaties.

2. To work in the meantime by all means for reducing the prices of industrial goods, not by increasing the import of goods from abroad but by the development of our domestic production, which makes mandatory the influx of foreign capital.

3. To postpone a lowering of our tariff until the time of the renewal of our trade treaties, so that, in turn, we can insist upon favorable terms for our agricultural exports.

4. Not to impose in the meantime new restraints on the influx of foreign capital, either through new laws or new interpretations of existing laws or, *especially, through administrative decrees.*

5. To maintain unchanged our present policy toward foreign capital until 1904, so that with its help our domestic industries can develop in the meantime to a position of such strength that in the renewal of trade treaties we may be able to make genuine reductions on several of our tariff rates.

6. To review in 1904, at the time of the renewal of the trade treaties, the problem of foreign capital and to decide then whether new safeguards should be added to existing legislation.

In submitting this program to favorable consideration by Your Imperial Highness, I respectfully ask that it may please you, my sovereign, to make certain that it may not be endangered henceforth by waverings and changes, because our industries, and our national economy in general, require a firm and consistent system carried to its conclusion.

If this program does not find the support of Your Imperial Highness, then, pray, tell me which economic policy I am to pursue.

STATE SECRETARY S. TU. WITTE

III/22/1899

Stolypin: To Save the Crown Suppress Revolutionaries and Create Individual Peasant Landowners

LEONID I. STRAKHOVSKY

Russian-born, Leonid Strakhovsky (1898–1963) was for many years a professor of history at Georgetown and Maryland Universities and later at the University of Toronto. His principal historical works are distinguished by strong monarchist and conservative feelings and by a conviction that the world should be told some of the facts about Russian affairs which Communist and other revolutionary groups have deliberately distorted or suppressed. His analysis of Stolypin, reprinted in part here, heavily stresses the positive aspects of Stolypin's administration and places an extremely sympathetic emphasis upon the intelligence, courage and noble purpose of the man whom revolutionaries considered a murderous, dangerously effective defender of autocracy.

PETER Arkadiyevich Stolypin came from an old and distinguished family of landed nobility. His father, a hero of the defence of Sebastopol in the Crimean war and later commander of an army corps in the Russo-Turkish war of 1877–8, ended his career as governor of the Kremlin. His mother was born a Princess Gorchakov, belonging to one of the most illustrious families of Russia. He was born in 1862 in Dresden but spent his childhood on the family estate near Moscow. After completing his secondary-school studies in Moscow he entered the University of St. Petersburg. Having been always intensely interested in agriculture and in the lot of the Russian peasant, he chose to study agriculture in the department of natural sciences. While still a student at the university, he married Olga Neidhart, daughter of the grand marshal of the court.

After graduating from the university in 1885, Stolypin served two years in the ministry of state domains. Then in 1887 he was appointed county marshal of nobility in the province of Kovno, where he possessed an estate. During ten years in this office he worked ceaselessly to improve the conditions of the peasants in his county. When he was appointed provincial marshal of nobility he had a larger field before him. He organised the Kovno association for agriculture in order to co-ordinate the efforts of the three leading national groups in the

From Leonid Strakhovsky, "The Statesmanship of Peter Stolypin: A Reappraisal," *The Slavonic and East European Review*, XXXVII (June 1959), pp. 349–52, 356–69. By permission of Florence C. Strakhovsky and *The Slavonic and East European Review*.

province: Russians, Poles, and Lithuanians. When he was appointed governor of the neighbouring province of Grodno in 1902, one of his first acts was to present his own programme for agrarian reform at the opening session of the committee for the relief of peasants. The main objectives of this programme were to encourage and develop individual peasant ownership of land, to abolish the communal redistribution of land, and to create and extend credit facilities for the peasants. This was in essence the agrarian reform which he carried out four years later when he was at the head of the Russian government. In this committee he had already to combat the reactionaries who wanted to prevent the education of the peasants. Stolypin spoke out boldly:

> One should not be afraid of education or of enlightenment. . . . Our country has a great need for the education of women. The spread of agricultural knowledge, which no country can afford to deny, depends on general education; the country which is lacking in it will go to ruin. Spread education and you will consolidate the agricultural class which is the most conservative of all classes in the entire world.

These ideas remained with him throughout his career. . . .

. . . In 1904 he had sent a lengthy personal report to Nicholas II in which he discussed in detail his ideas about the emancipation of the peasants from the village commune. This report, as well as the record of his firm policy in suppressing revolutionary activities, induced the tsar to call him to office, apparently upon the recommendation of the then prime minister, I. L. Goremykin. On 5 May 1906, Stolypin was appointed minister of the interior, which post controlled both the regular and the secret police and was considered to be the most important cabinet office after that of the prime minister. . . .

It was a difficult time. Russia seethed with revolt, and the first Duma definitely favoured revolution. As Sir Bernard Pares has remarked:

> The only cabinet minister who knew how to face the Duma was Mr. Stolypin. He answered interpolations with the utmost moderation, but with the utmost firmness; and once, when the labour group tried to shout him down, he turned on them and addressed the rest of his speech to them in a voice which rose loud and strong above all their clamour. He was the one minister who was ever cheered by any member of the Duma.

His success in dealing with the Duma prompted the tsar to appoint him prime minister on 21 July 1906, while he still retained the portfolio of minister of the interior. It was the tsar's personal decision, and it came as a complete surprise not only to Stolypin but also to Goremykin, whom he was to replace as head of the government. To complicate matters, the tsar had decided to dissolve the Duma when announcing the change of government. Stolypin definitely dissociated himself from the reactionaries who surrounded the throne, yet he had no choice but to accept his sovereign's command. However, at an audience with the tsar on 23 July 1906, he stated two conditions upon which he would accept the premiership: first, the immediate dismissal of two ministers who had made themselves conspicuously odious by their reactionary tendencies and a free hand for a further reshuffling of the cabinet; second, the eventual formation of a coalition government which was to include members of the opposition. The tsar granted these conditions and noted in his diary: "I received Stolypin; from his first steps I obtained the best impression." . . .

During his five years in office he was the most hunted man in Russia. And while as a person he could face danger with courage and equanimity, as the head of the government he had to act boldly and decisively to stem the spread of revolutionary terror. This terror was directed not only against the high officials of the government, the court, the army and navy, but also against the rank and file of government employees, officers, and even ordinary policemen. Thus, from November 1905 to June 1906, from among the employees of the ministry of the interior alone 288 persons were killed and 383 wounded, while 156 others were attacked but escaped injury. Up to the end of October 1906 a total of 3,611 government officials of all ranks had been killed or wounded. The need for stern measures was pressing. This was realised by the tsar himself, who sent a message to Stolypin on 27 August 1906: "I command the council of ministers to inform me without delay what measures it considers most adequate to undertake in order to carry out my immovable will to uproot rebellion and to re-establish order." To this he added in a postscript: "It seems that only an extraordinary law, promulgated as a temporary measure until peace and quiet are re-established, could give assurance that the government had undertaken decisive measures and would thus quiet everyone."

In fulfilment of this command, Stolypin enacted on 1 September, with the approval of his entire cabinet, the establishment of field courts martial and gave discretionary powers to governors-general to have terrorists tried by military courts, often without due process of law. All told, from the day of their institution until their abolition on 3 May 1907, these field courts martial sentenced to death and had executed 1,144 persons. In addition, 329 persons were sentenced to hard labour, 443 to imprisonment for different lengths of time, and 7 to exile, while 71 were acquitted. The law establishing them was promulgated under article 87 of the fundamental laws which gave the government the right to enact legislation in the interval between Duma sessions subject to approval by the next Duma. It was permitted to lapse, because the government did not present it for the approval of the second Duma since it was certain of rejection. But terrorist activity continued long after the abolition of field courts martial, though it slackened after 1907. According to figures given by Stolypin himself in an interview with Gaston Dru, a French journalist, 738 officials and 645 private persons were killed during 1906, while 948 officials and 777 private persons were wounded. In 1907 no fewer than 1,231 officials and 1,768 private persons were killed and 1,284 officials and 1,734 private persons were wounded. But in 1908 the number of officials killed fell sharply to 365 and the number of officials wounded to 571. The number of private persons killed and wounded also fell to 1,349 and 1,384. An opponent of the government states that during July 1907, no fewer than 54 government officials were killed; among them were 2 governors of provinces, 3 county police officers, 2 deputy county police officers, 1 commander of a regiment, 1 assistant prison warden, 1 judge, 19 policemen, etc. During the same month 47 officials were wounded; seven attempts at assassination failed; 95 private persons, mostly bystanders, were killed; and armed robberies for political purposes yielded 400,000 rubles, of which 270,000 rubles of government funds were mostly from post-offices and drink shops. However, in January 1908 only 20 government officials were killed and 47 wounded, while private persons lost 48 killed and 47 wounded. Armed robberies also decreased to the amount of 52,700 rubles.

In a government declaration of 6 September 1906, Stolypin justified the use of article 87 not only for the establishment of field courts martial but also for the enactment of much-needed reforms. All told in the interval between the first and second Dumas, he enacted 59 important laws under the authority of article 87. Interestingly enough he received complete support for all these actions from A. I. Guchkov, leader of the octobrists, who had refused to enter his cabinet and who now declared in an interview:

I have absolute confidence in Stolypin; until now we have not had such talented and capable persons as he at the seat of power. I am convinced that he will apply all his efforts for the realisation of his programme. I believe in the purity of his intentions and in his ardent love for our poor martyred fatherland, but everything will depend on the extent of his authority. The fulfilment of the promises which he has made in his declaration will be possible only if he has sufficient power to carry them out.

For the time being at least Stolypin had the confidence and support of the tsar, hence the power to carry out his programme.

As a preliminary measure to his far-reaching land reform, Stolypin obtained the consent of the tsar for the transfer of appanage lands to the peasant land bank for sale among the land-short peasants. This was enacted on 25 August 1906, the very day he almost became the victim of revolutionary terrorists. On 9 September state lands were added to the funds of the peasant land bank. On 18 October, a decree abolished the last vestiges of serfdom: the peasants were equalised with other classes in their rights and became eligible for offices in the local administration, some of which were made elective. Also they could no longer be punished by land captains without trial. Finally, on 22 November 1906, Stolypin enacted his famous agrarian law which followed his fundamental idea of liberating the individual peasant from the stranglehold of the village commune.

The peasant problem in Russia at that time was twofold: first, the antiquated system of leaving one-third of the land fallow every year reduced the general over-all yield; secondly, a thrifty and enterprising peasant, as a member of a village commune, held his land not in ownership but in tenure and subject to redistribution, which precluded any initiative on his part to improve his holding lest it be given to someone else in the commune. He was also forced by the community to adhere to the three-field system. Hence the yield of peasant communal land was from 15 to 20 per cent lower than that of privately owned land and from three to four times lower than in most other European countries. And since in 1905 in European Russia, which was the most densely populated part of the country, the peasants owned 443 million acres as against 143 million acres (of which much was forest) belonging to the nobility, it was not so much the quantity of peasant land that was the problem as the quality of its exploitation. Actually the Russian peasant was much better off than his counterpart in Western Europe. In European Russia there were 5.7 acres of convenient arable land per person, but in France only 2.21 acres, in Germany 1.67 acres and in Great Britain 1.3 acres. But the radical parties and their allies — the constitutional democrats — disregarded these facts and demanded a redistribution of land at the expense of the landed nobility.

Projects for nationalisation, socialisation, and municipalisation of land had been introduced in the first Duma, but they were all impracticable. As a Russian economist remarks:

Considering that the peasants, as a class, were already the largest landowners in Russia and that, of state lands and large estates, the greater part by far consisted of forests and only a relatively very small proportion could be transferred to the peasants as arable, these measures could not improve the position of the peasants to any marked extent.

When defending his agrarian law later in the second Duma, Stolypin pointed out that if all the land of whatever kind was divided among the peasants, each peasant household would possess in the fourteen central provinces of European Russia less than forty acres and in some provinces only twenty-one. Furthermore, the increase of population among the peasants in European Russia alone amounted to 1,625,000 a year, which would necessitate the provision yearly of nine and a half million acres if each newcomer was to have an average-sized holding; but there were no such reserves of land in Russia. Hence Stolypin's agrarian law backed the thrifty and industrious peasant by offering to him new opportunities and the right to own his land, and took it for granted that the lazy and indolent elements in the peasant class would either be eliminated altogether or driven into the ranks of urban workers, since the growing industries of Russia demanded more and more labour. This process of transforming peasants into urban workers was already then quite far advanced.

The law of 22 November tackled practically every aspect of the agrarian problem. It set out in the first instance to improve the conditions of peasant farming by the substitution of compact enclosed freehold farms for the existing medley of agricultural units held communally by the village. It also provided for the improvement of the system of tenure on lands remaining in communal ownership by helping the peasants to eliminate inconveniences caused by the jumbling together of lands assigned to different individuals. It included the provision of technical and financial assistance to peasant farmers for the improvement of their holdings and cultivation. Through the peasant land bank, whose statute was revised so as to enable it greatly to extend its operations, mainly for the benefit of the poorer peasantry, Stolypin's agrarian law helped the peasants to buy more land on liberal conditions of credit, thus inaugurating a scheme of widespread internal colonisation. Last, but not least, it opened up Asiatic Russia to surplus population by developing a system of assisted migration on a large scale into the south-eastern steppes and organising the colonisation of Siberia.

Thus, whilst striking at the revolutionaries, Stolypin was also striving to foster a strong peasant democracy. No wonder the parties of the left saw in this double policy a threat to their very existence since a strong independent class of peasant farmers would have been a bulwark against revolution. Lenin, while calling this legislation "a progressive one in the scientific-economic sense," and recognising that it would provide "the quickest development of productive forces, the best conditions of labour for the mass of the population," attacked it tooth and nail because he realised that its success would spell the doom of revolution in Russia. "Stolypin understood the situation correctly: without breaking up the old system of land-ownership one cannot guarantee the economic development of Russia." But while recognising the possibility of success for Stolypin's measure, Lenin stubbornly exclaimed: "The Social-Democratic Workers' Party will continue to explain, to propagate the idea that a joint uprising of the peasants with the proletariat is the *only* possible means to prevent Stolypin's method of 'rejuvenating' Russia from succeeding."

Stolypin presented his agrarian legislation, as demanded by law, to the second Duma where it was subjected to severe criticism not only from the revolutionary parties but from the constitutional democrats as well. But among the latter there were a few who were not blinded by their hatred for the prime minister. Among these was V. A. Maklakov, a member of the right wing of the party elected from Moscow, who said at a political meeting: "Stolypin places his stake on strong homesteaders; our party — on landless peasants by means of providing them with land expropriated from the landlords. Who is right? the future will tell; but if Stolypin is right, God speed him."

On 23 May 1907 Stolypin addressed the second Duma in defence of his legislation. He ended his speech by saying:

> Having spent about ten years in close touch with the agrarian needs of the nation, I have come to the conclusion that the solution of these problems demands untiring effort and long and tedious spade work. It is impossible to solve these problems now and outright; their solution will take time. In Western European countries it took decades. We offer you a modest, but sure way. The enemies of statesmanship would like to choose the road of radicalism, the road which leads to the severance of ties with Russia's historical past, with her cultural tradition. They want great upheavals, but we want a great Russia.

But the "enemies of statesmanship" failed to listen to reason and debated the legislation, without taking action, until the second Duma was dissolved. It was only in the third Duma on 7 May 1909 that the agrarian reform was passed by a majority of the centre and moderate right against all parties of the left, the constitutional democrats, and the extreme right.

Now came the turn of the council of state. Here the main opposition came from the right, which looked upon communal ownership not only as traditional but also as inherently Russian, giving protection to the weaker elements in the peasant community. The opposition expressed fear that compulsion was used in the breaking up of the village commune. On 28 March 1910 Stolypin addressed the council of state and said in part:

This law has not only been verified by the theoretical discussions of specialists, it is being verified by life itself. During the three years that the provisions of this law have been in operation, i.e., up to 1 February 1910, over 1,700,000 heads of families have declared their desire to obtain their land in private ownership. This represents about 17 per cent of all peasants in village communes. I have too great a respect for people's wisdom to admit that the Russian peasantry is reorganising its land habits by order and not by inner conviction.

Consequently the law was passed by the council of state and on 27 June 1910 it was signed by the tsar. It was incorporated in the code of laws as the statute for land settlement on 11 June 1911, and thus became one of the fundamental laws.

These dates show clearly what a long battle Stolypin had to wage for his agrarian reform. But the results were encouraging. By the time of the enactment of the law, over two and a half million heads of families had given formal notification of their desire to leave the commune; and by the end of 1914 nearly two million heads of families enjoyed private land-ownership, while an additional half-million had received certificates entitling them to ownership of their communal lots in villages where there had not been a redistribution of land for the last twenty years. All told, this represented over 25 per cent of peasants in village communes. . . .

Stolypin followed his agrarian reform with other measures. On 28 November 1906 rules were published establishing "normal rest" for employees in commercial and craft establishments, shops, and offices. This was followed by the granting of freedom of worship to the Old Believers and other dissenters from the Orthodox Church. But when Stolypin tried to remove some of the restrictions most irksome to the Jewish population of Russia he was stopped by the tsar himself, who returned unsigned on 23 December 1906 a recommendation of the council of ministers to ameliorate the position of Jews, explaining in a personal letter to Stolypin:

Despite most convincing arguments in favour of adopting a positive decision in this matter, an inner voice keeps on insisting more and more that I do not accept responsibility for it. So far my conscience has not deceived me. Therefore I intend in this case also to follow its dictates.

Two days earlier, on 21 December, an imperial decree called for elections to the second Duma on 19 February 1907. Although Stolypin's ministry had imposed some new restrictions on the electors by legal means, such as by decisions of the governing senate, it let the electoral campaign proceed in complete freedom, hoping that the vast majority of the electors would recognise the undoubted benefits of the legislation passed since the dissolution of the first Duma. But the results were unexpected. While the centre lost its predominant position, the extremes on the left and on the right gained. Consequently, Stolypin had to face an unfriendly legislative body.

The opening of the second Duma was fixed for 5 March 1907. In order not to repeat the error of the preceding government and let the new assembly waste its time in sterile declamations, Stolypin had prepared a vast legislative programme. In addition to the agrarian law, it included legislation concerning religious liberty, *habeas corpus,* civic equality, state insurance for the benefit of the working classes, an income tax bill, reform of the *zemstva,* establishment of *zemstva* in the Baltic provinces and Poland where they did not then exist, and reform of local tribunals, of higher and secondary schools, and of the police. But the Duma was in an ugly mood. At the opening session, during the reading of the imperial decree calling it into being, the whole left including the constitutional democrats remained seated. This was meant to be an expression of their opposition, but actually, of course, was merely bad manners.

On 19 March, two weeks after the second Duma opened, Stolypin read the government declaration outlining his entire programme for the immediate future. He was followed on the tribune by Tseretelli, a menshevik, who delivered a fiery speech, which was an outright appeal for revolution, full of hatred toward the government and constituted authority. Other orators from the left added their bit to the fire, while the protests of the right transformed the meeting into bedlam, which was quieted only by a recess. After the Duma reconvened, Stolypin demanded to be heard. He was a born orator; the historic speech he delivered had not been prepared. It was brief but breathed such force and such dignity that no disrespectful shout was heard during its delivery. After stating that the government would like to find a common ground and language with the Duma and that there was no place for hatred in common work, he ended with these words:

All these attacks are intended to cause a paralysis of will and thought in the government and the executive; they can be summed up in two words addressed to the authorities: 'Hands up!' To these words, gentlemen, the government, confident in its righteousness, can answer calmly with only two other words: 'Not afraid!'

* * *

During the time of the third Duma, Stolypin had only one major setback and it came from the right but not in the Duma. On 17 March 1910 the council of state, led by a bloc of reactionary landowners, voted down a law for the introduction of *zemstva* in Poland which had been previously passed by the Duma. This action sought to avoid the imposition of heavier taxes on large estates and to prevent the development of progressive and liberal ideas which thrived in these autonomous bodies, as experience in other parts of Russia had proved. The day after this rejection of one of his major reforms by the upper chamber, Stolypin tendered his resignation to the tsar.

At first the tsar seemed inclined to accept the resignation of his prime minister; but the energetic intervention of his cousins, Grand Dukes Nicholas Mikhaylovich and Alexander Mikhaylovich, the latter being also his brother-in-law because he was married to the tsar's sister Xenia, and finally that of his mother, led him to change his mind [and to request Stolypin to withdraw his resignation]. . . .

Stolypin complied with the tsar's request, but consented to remain as head of the government only on condition that, first, the Duma and the council of state should immediately be prorogued for three days so that he could put into effect the introduction of *zemstva* in Poland under the provision of article 87 and, secondly, that the two leaders of the right-wing opposition in the council of state — Durnovo and Trepov — be sent on leave of absence until the end of the year. The tsar agreed to these demands of his prime minister, but not satisfied with an oral promise, Stolypin requested that the sovereign should write these conditions down, which Nicholas II did in his own hand in blue pencil on a large sheet of paper. "I saw this sheet with my own eyes," wrote Shidlovsky, a prominent octobrist member of the third Duma, "when Stolypin showed it to me."

Consequently on 25 March 1910 the legislative chambers were prorogued for three days, during which the law establishing *zemstva* in Poland was promulgated under article 87. Both the Duma, which had adopted the law, and the council of state, which had rejected it, were incensed at this high-handedness on Stolypin's part. They demonstrated their opposition to the prime minister at Durnovo's departure abroad, when at the railway station almost all members of the council of state and many members of the Duma of all political parties participated in an imposing farewell.

Stolypin was the victor, but it was a Pyrrhic victory. He alienated the Duma, which feared that the disregard of the constitutional prerogatives of the council of state could be also applied to it at some time. Needless to say, he alienated the council of state where even moderate members now looked on him with suspicion and enmity. Finally, the tsar never forgave Stolypin the distrust shown in his word when Stolypin requested a written confirmation of the sovereign's consent. "Perhaps in this case Stolypin was right," wrote Shidlovsky, "but tsars never forgive such distrust." Hence hereafter Stolypin could not work as before with the three sources of power in the country: the tsar, the Duma, and the council of state. . . .

After this event, Stolypin's power and influence were never the same as before. His health too was undermined and breaking down. And when in September 1911 he went to Kiev to attend the ceremonies of the unveiling of a monument to Alexander II in the presence of the tsar and the members of his family, he was a sick man, as revealed later by the autopsy; but he felt it his duty to be present not only as head of the government but also because delegates of the newly elected *zemstva* of Poland, which had been established thanks to his rather unorthodox determination, were to be presented to Nicholas II. Although he had previously been rewarded with a high court title, he was irked at Kiev by his sovereign's inattention. And there on the evening of 14 September 1911, while attending a performance of Rimsky-Korsakov's opera *Tsar' Saltan* in the presence of the tsar and his family he was shot twice and mortally wounded by Mordka Bogrov, a Jewish revolutionary who, paradoxically, also served as an agent of the Russian secret police. Before he slumped into his chair in the front row of the stalls, he turned toward the imperial box and made the sign of the cross in its direction, thus imparting his blessing upon the sovereign to whom he was devoted, even though he did not always trust him, but who by then did not have any confidence or trust in the one man who could have saved the Russian monarchy from the catastrophe which was to come. Five days later he died. . . .

PROGRESS IN MODERNIZATION

The Agrarian Situation Was Improving

LAZAR VOLIN

For many years Lazar Volin has been a specialist in the field of Soviet economics for the United States Department of Agriculture, where he is at present Chief of the Eastern European Branch. He is the author of *A Survey of Soviet Russian Agriculture* (1951) and many shorter studies. In the selection presented below, while analyzing the causes of peasant dissatisfaction after 1861, Volin emphasizes the beneficial changes introduced after 1905 and concludes that the agrarian problem might very well have been solved without revolution.

I

THE period between 1861 and the revolution of 1917 poses a crucial question: why, having begun with a promising agrarian reform, did it end with a peasant revolt resembling in many respects Pushkin's celebrated "Russian mutiny — terrible and senseless"? Certainly Alexander II recognized the dilemma — agrarian reform or eventual revolution — when he warned the serf-owning landlords in the beginning of his reign that it is better to liberate serfs from above than to wait until they liberated themselves. He saw the handwriting on the wall and hoped to forestall a possible peasant uprising, a rumbling of which was to be heard in frequent local mutinies of serfs, keeping alive that nightmare of the serf-owner — the *Pugachevshchina*.[1] When the government's intention to abolish serfdom became known about a hundred years ago, it was greeted with immense enthusiasm by the Russian intelligentsia of all shades of opinion: from the Slavophiles at the right, to liberals like Kavelin and (at that time) Katkov at the center, to Herzen at the left of center, and even Chernyshevsky at the extreme left.

This enthusiasm, however, faded as the emancipation legislation, which was to affect so profoundly the life of the liberated peasantry, began to take shape. Not only did radicals like Ogarev and Chernyshevsky damn the emancipation reform, but even Ivan Aksakov, the conservative Slavophile, was critical. For a strong impact was exerted on the new legislation by the landowning nobility, which was strongly entrenched at the imperial court and in the governing bureaucracy. The landowners were bent on making the liberation process

[1] A term for a peasant revolt derived from the name of Emelian Pugachev, the leader of a formidable peasant rebellion in the 1770's during the reign of Catherine the Great.

Reprinted by permission of the publishers from the article by Lazar Volin, "The Russian Peasant: From Emancipation to Kolkhoz," in C. E. Black (ed.), *The Transformation of Russian Society*, Cambridge, Mass.: Harvard University Press, pp. 293–304.

economically as painless as possible to themselves when they realized its inevitability. The pressure of the landlord interests, though in some respects divergent (as between different geographic regions), resulted in many a compromise unfavorable to the liberated peasants.[2]

To be sure, the peasant ceased to be legally what Herzen called "baptized property." And, what is equally important in view of the attachment of the Russian peasants to their land, they were not liberated as landless proletarians. This was the fate of the peasants freed from bondage much earlier in the Baltic provinces (1818), and the idea was toyed with during the early preparatory stage of the emancipation reform but later abandoned.

The peasants did not obtain all the land they hoped for in accordance with the strongly implanted concept that land should belong to those who toil on it. Actually, the landowning nobility retained about 45 per cent of the best land.[3] In the allotment of the remainder to the more than 20 million peasants, however, there were considerable regional variations, dictated by the divergent interests of the landowning gentry in different areas.

A large section of the liberated peasantry in the more fertile regions, where land was valuable, was allotted even a smaller area than it had tilled for its own needs under serfdom. The holdings allotted were also often of poor quality and location, and lacking such important components as meadows (hayland) and woodland, necessitating the leasing of these types of land from the former master. In these and other aspects of the land-allotment process was the genesis of the continued economic dependence of the liberated peasants on their former master which persisted long after the emancipation. Here was a source of irritation and conflict which poisoned the liberated peasant-landlord relations.

The situation was aggravated by the financial aspects of the emancipation reform. The peasants were saddled with a heavy redemption price for the allotted land that exceeded its market value before allotment. The fiscal burden of redemption payments and taxes, sometimes even exceeding the income from land, began early to figure as one of the chief causes of rural destitution in the findings of official investigating commissions and of private investigators and observers during the post-emancipation era. Moreover, fiscal considerations involved in the task of extracting the burdensome redemption payments and taxes were, to a large extent, responsible for the fact that the peasant was not made an independent land proprietor or full-fledged citizen and that his mobility was restricted.

Thus, over a large part of the country, ownership of peasant land was vested in the whole village community or mir and not held as private property in fee simple by the individual peasant farmer. The mir apportioned the land on some egalitarian basis to the peasant family or household (*krest'ianskii dvor*), which was the actual farm unit. The latter could not even refuse to accept an allotment, however unprofitable. For taxes had to be paid under a system of unlimited responsibility of the whole membership — whether the land was tilled or not. Incidentally, the legal restrictions with which the allotted land was hedged and segregated from other privately owned

[2] The divergence was principally between the landowners of the more fertile regions of the black-soil area, where land itself was the most valuable element of the estate economy, and the much less fertile nonblack-soil area, where the landowners to a large extent derived their income not from farming of their own, but from quit-rents paid by the serfs, who gained their livelihood partly from agriculture and partly from nonagricultural pursuits.

[3] The reduction of the land area allotted to peasants after the emancipation amounted to 9.9 per cent in 15 nonblack-soil provinces and 26.2 per cent in 21 black-soil provinces, and 18.1 per cent for the combined 36 provinces. In some provinces the reduction exceeded 30 to 40 per cent. It should be noted, however, that in addition to the more than 20 million private serfs there were also the so-called crown (state) peasants and those belonging to the imperial family, numbering altogether close to 20 million. These categories fared much better and suffered no reduction of their land area.

land were further tightened by the law of December 14, 1893.

The mir also assumed much of the police authority over the peasants which was formerly exercised by the landlords, including the power of deportation to Siberia. It shared with the heads of the households the important power to grant or withhold permission to obtain and renew the much-coveted passport, without which a peasant could not leave his native village for any length of time. It was, however, mainly the persistent and vexing tax arrears which led to intervention of the mir in the affairs of the individual household. To ensure payment, a member of the defaulting household could be hired out or the head of the household could be removed and a different member appointed in his place.

Thus the mir, usually under the leadership of its more prosperous or more aggressive elements, lorded it over the average peasant. In turn, the mir and the volost (a unit of rural self-government which comprised several village communities) were dominated by government officials, whose legal power of interference was increased during the latter part of the nineteenth century. The elected peasant aldermen were "elective in name only and depend to such an extent on the local government bureaucracy that they cannot even think about defending the interests of their community. As a result the better element of the village as a rule shuns service and the positions are occupied by the scum of the peasant population." Such was the testimony gathered from various sources by an investigation at the beginning of the century.

The peasants also had separate lower courts, where minor criminal and civil cases were tried in accordance with custom law. This "very often proved to be no law at all," so ill-defined and unfairly and arbitrarily administered was it. The quality of the village judges was no better than that of other elective officials, who were tools of the *chinovniki* (government officials). Corporal punishment was retained in these peasant courts long after it was abolished in the penal system of the general courts, which had undergone a thorough and highly progressive reform in the 1860's.

Still another set of limitations to which the peasants, but not other classes of the population, were subjected stemmed from the customary joint family ownership of the property of a peasant household, which was retained after the emancipation. While it protected individual members against the improvidence of the head of the household, it also had disadvantages for the individual. For instance, all his earnings from whatsoever source were supposed to go into the common pool — a serious matter, considering the prevalence of migratory work in the overpopulated Russian village. Even peasants who had long lived and worked away from the village were often forced to continue their contributions to the household of which they legally remained members. The weapon here was the famous Russian passport, which hung like the sword of Damocles over the head of any peasant who wanted to live away from his native village.

Despite the various restrictions the traditional Great Russian large peasant family began to feel the disintegrating impact of individualism following the emancipation. This was manifested in numerous family divisions, notwithstanding certain economic advantages possessed by a large peasant family. In the 1880's the government became so alarmed over the adverse effects of family divisions that it tried to restrain them by law. Such restraint, however, was unavailing and served only to provide an additional source of vexation to the peasant.

This all adds up to a picture of the liberated Russian peasantry remaining "a peasant nation consistently segregated from the general life of the community (state)," instead of being drawn closer to the rest of the citizenry. Such a view has not been seriously challenged. Writing fifty years later, as moderate a political thinker as V. A. Maklakov likened the postemancipation status of the Russian peasant to a "kind of caste" — an oppressed caste, we may add — lorded over by the chinovniki and their stooges.

The segregation or insulation of the peasant class was enhanced by the growing cultural lag between the town and the country. Culturally, urban Russia made great strides during the second half of the nineteenth century with a significant democratization and broadening of the predominantly upper-class culture. But this progress hardly touched the Russian village, which continued to live in ignorance. Precious little was done by the Tsarist government even to stamp out wholesale illiteracy until the revolution of 1905. On the contrary, it did its best to hamper the educational and cultural activities undertaken by the local self-government (zemstvo), private organizations, and public-spirited individuals. The government attitude was summed up by a well-known authority, N. N. Kovalevsky, as follows:

> The principal objective of the government was not to spread popular education as widely and as rapidly as possible, but to ward off some kind of a danger to the nation because the people will acquire too much knowledge unnecessarily through schools and books, and will broaden their intellectual horizon. There are still not a few persons who are convinced that popular ignorance is the best guarantee of social order.

"The access of peasants to books was hindered to the utmost by the authorities; lectures and talks in the village, even when dealing with strictly specialized subjects, met actually almost insurmountable obstacles," wrote the eminent Russian economist and educator, A. A. Manuilov.

It was the consensus of experts and observers of Russian rural conditions at the turn of the century that the legal, social, and cultural isolation and ignorance of the liberated peasantry failed to develop its power of initiative, stifled the spirit of enterprise, and tended to reinforce the natural inertia. Thus it also contributed to the growing economic destitution caused by the inadequate land allotment in many areas and aggravated by a rapidly growing population and heavy fiscal burdens. This situation was complicated by a transition from a self-sufficient to a money economy and by inadequate outlets for the surplus manpower. These were lacking because of slow industrial development, failure to encourage agricultural resettlement, legal restrictions on mobility, and insufficient improvement and intensification of agricultural techniques. The latter process was, in turn, retarded by peasant poverty and the consequent shortage of capital, inadequate markets for farm products, lack of know-how, cultural backwardness of the farm population, and lack of agronomic assistance.

The idea that all was not well with emancipated rural Russia began to gain ground in the public mind soon after the emancipation reform. As a matter of fact, as we saw above, serious criticism of the reform began with its very proclamation. A decade later, in 1872, an official commission of inquiry into rural conditions was set up, the Valuev Commission, before which much pessimistic testimony was given. Twenty years later, following the catastrophic famine in 1891, an even gloomier view that the Russian village was in the throes of a serious crisis because of increasing impoverishment gained wide acceptance. The paradox of a chronic undernourishment of the farm population in a country which had become one of the leading exporters of grain and other foodstuffs was stressed by numerous observers and witnesses before the official investigating commissions, such as that established under the chairmanship of the Minister of Finance, Count Witte. The increase in the number of peasant households without work horses and the generally poor condition of peasant livestock lacking an adequate feed-supply base, the increasing parceling of peasant holdings, the piling up of tax arrears — these were some of the symptoms of the growing deterioration of peasant agriculture.

If the peasant could still, with some difficulty, keep his head above water in years of good or average harvests, he was faced with disaster when crops failed, as they often did, especially in the large semiarid belt of Russia. Famine conditions, epidemics, increased mortality, decrease in the number of livestock (including work horses which, by striking at the sole source of farm power, did more than anything else to undermine the very foundation of peasant farming) — this is the spectacle of the growing destitution of a famine-stricken Russian village. The adverse effects of such conditions were felt long after the worst of the famine had passed. What Kipling wrote of the Indian peasant in the 1890's could be applied to his Russian counterpart as well: "His life is a long-drawn question between a crop and a crop."

The chronic rural distress should not obscure the fact that there always had been a small group which was economically better off than the great mass of the peasants. Leadership in the village and also a tendency to exploit the poorer peasants through usurious loans, and such, was often characteristic of this group. Such economic stratification in the village was noted, for instance, as early as the 1870's by the astute observer, A. N. Engel'gardt, in his celebrated *Letters from the Village* which, incidentally, can still be read with much interest and were recently republished by the Soviets. But growing economic stratification in the village was particularly stressed by Marxist socialist writers, who appeared on the scene in the 1880's. At that time a split took place in the Russian socialist movement between the new orthodox Marxist wing and the older populist (*narodnik*) or agrarian-minded current which based its socialist ideology on the peasant mir and not on the industrial proletariat. A vigorous controversy developed between the Marxists and the populists concerning the trend of economic development of Russia and, more specifically, the inevitability of its passing through a capitalist stage. The populists took a dim view of this. The Marxists, on the contrary, found supporting evidence for their traditional analysis of economic development (which postulates class stratification and polarization concomitant with the growth of capitalism) in the stratification process taking place in the Russian village. They claimed that the mir system with its egalitarian tendency of land tenure retarded but did not eliminate this process. However, in their preoccupation with economics, the Marxists neglected other influences in rural stratification, notably the demographic factor — that is, the composition and the size of the family. These, as Kaufman, Chaianov, and others showed, played an important role in the process of village stratification. Larger and stronger peasant holdings were usually associated with larger families, and vice versa.[4]

The public discussion of the agrarian question and the toil of scholars and official investigating commissions produced copious and highly valuable material on rural conditions in Russia for which a student of Russian agrarian history must be eternally grateful. But they did not result in any serious corrective measures until the revolution of 1905. To be sure, the peasant had the active sympathy of the progressive Russian intelligentsia which considered it a sacred duty to help the poverty-stricken masses. As ill-paid doctors, teachers, nurses, and zemstvo workers, the intellectuals threw themselves unsparingly into this work, undeterred by the discouraging opposition and persecution of the government. Famine relief especially brought out strenuous efforts by the intelligentsia on behalf of the stricken population. But all this devotion was a drop in the ocean of peasant need. However, it greatly helped to keep the issue in the public spotlight. And so did the sympathetic interest in the peasant by the Russian literature of the pre-Soviet

[4] The larger the family, the greater as a rule the number of workers as well as of the mouths to be fed. This meant that more land could be and needed to be taken on from the mir or leased from the neighboring estate or fellow peasants. If a large peasant family, however, was short of work horses or farm equipment, some of its workhands could seek employment in the city and, with the money thus earned, purchase the needed draft animals and implements.

era, imbued with a strong humanitarian tradition.

The more radical populist section of the intelligentsia also tried, against great odds, to arouse the peasantry by spreading socialist propaganda in the villages. It considered the Russian peasant partly prepared to embrace socialism because it detected a socialist germ in the institution of peasant communal land tenure, the mir, to which even Karl Marx gave qualified approval. But this socialist propaganda, even if it had not been quickly suppressed by the government, proved an abysmal failure. The peasants were not interested in socialism.

"What will you do," one of the propagandists (Zheliabov) asked a peasant whom he thought entirely converted to the socialist doctrine, "if you should get some five hundred rubles?" "Well, I will open a saloon," said the peasant.

And what about the peasant's attitude toward the crisis? What was his solution? It could be summed up in two words: "more land." He saw the root of all his difficulties in a shortage of land and his only salvation in extension of the cultivated area. It was easier, of course, to continue the same type of farming in a larger area than to reorganize the system of farming on the old holdings, especially when capital and knowledge were lacking. Moreover, some holdings were too small for any practicable improvement of farming. There were also historical and psychological reasons for the peasants' attitude. There was the traditional view that only the tillers of the soil were entitled to land; hence the disappointment of the peasants when they did not obtain all the estate land after emancipation. What rankled most, however, was the loss of the land which they tilled as serfs on their own — the so-called *otrezki* (literally, cut-off land). Lenin sensed this feeling when he sought, as a means of enlisting the peasantry, the inclusion of a demand for restoration of *otrezki* in the platform of the Social Democratic Party.

While the peasants acquiesced in the new land arrangements more peacefully than the government expected, despite a number of local mutinies,[5] they never fully accepted them as a just solution. The peasants continued to dream, after emancipation, of a new partition of land to be ordered by the kind tsar, once he was able to overcome the resistance of the nobles and his ministers. Naturally, as the crisis deepened, they looked with increasingly covetous eyes on the broad acres of the "nobles' nests" which adjoined their narrow strips. How he could lay his hands on this land, of which he considered himself unjustly deprived, became the central preoccupation of the Russian peasant.

There was another influence which tended to reinforce this peasant outlook with respect to estate land. This was again the mir. I shall not deal here with the intense controversy, historical, economic, and ideological, which this institution provoked and which did not cease until the revolution of 1917. I only want to call attention to the central feature of the repartitional mir system: the peasant family held its strips of land not permanently (except for the homestead and the attached kitchen garden), but only until the next repartition. Then the holding could change both in size and location. Such repartitions took place at regular or irregular intervals. If the land was given up for one reason or another by a member, it reverted to the mir, which had the right to redistribute it. But the member still retained his right to an allotment. In other words, the peasant had a right to a holding but not to a particular holding; and he could not sell it. The actual farming unit, however, was the individual peasant household and not the mir, just as the kolkhoz is at present.

The repartitions of land and physical changes in holdings kept alive in the peas-

[5] It was, however, by no means a submission without a protest, inasmuch as there were more than 1,100 cases of disorders and uprisings in different villages during the two years 1861–1863.

ant mind the idea of the egalitarian distribution of land in accordance with the dictates of rough primitive justice. And why should such egalitarianism stop at the boundary line that divided the allotted from the estate lands? The peasant mind, unaccustomed to legalistic niceties, saw no reason for such a segregation. With his peculiar concept of the right to land and the continuing practice of flexible landholding, the peasant considered the property right of the landlords less than sacrosanct.

II

Until 1905 the peasants, while constantly dreaming of a new partition to relieve their distress, were nevertheless resorting to legal means of allaying their land hunger. They purchased some estate lands and leased a much larger proportion, often on difficult terms. But as we saw, abundant explosive material was accumulating for a revolutionary conflagration in the village. The spark was provided by the outbreak of revolutionary disturbances in the cities in 1905, following the unpopular and unsuccessful war with Japan. Unrest, punctuated by numerous *jacqueries*, spread through the countryside. In the new Russian parliament, the Duma, in 1906 and 1907 the peasant deputies clamored for distribution of estate lands. And again, as during the emancipation reform half a century earlier, they were generally supported by all the progressive elements of Russian society. Even the moderate liberals, the Kadets, strongly advocated distribution of a major part of the estate lands with fair compensation of the landowners, in order to increase holdings of the poorer peasants. Many liberals acknowledged that such a land reform was no panacea for Russia's agrarian ills, which stemmed fundamentally from agricultural underproduction. But, with the peasant temper being what it was, this was a first inevitable step in the solution of a difficult problem. The government itself, when the revolutionary disturbances were at their height, toyed with the idea of a land reform, proposed by the Minister of Agriculture, N. N. Kutler. But as soon as it felt that it was riding out the revolutionary squall, the government, reflecting the aspirations of the majority of the landowning class, adamantly turned its back on all such schemes.

However, as an alternative to the radical and liberal proposals, P. A. Stolypin as prime minister (1906–1911) enacted his own kind of agrarian reform, epitomized by his famous slogan, a "wager on the strong." Its essence was to split the peasantry by the development of a class of independent, economically viable peasant proprietors who would be attached to the principle of private property, and therefore better coexist with the estate system and act as a bulwark against any future revolution in the village.

With this end in view, legislation was passed aiming at the breakdown of the mir and individualization of the peasant land tenure and other property relations. At the same time, much greater attention was paid by the government to technical progress in agriculture in its various aspects; much more was done in the way of technical and credit assistance to peasant farmers and encouragement of agricultural resettlement in Asiatic Russia. The redemption payments also ceased in 1907, while the gradual abolition of mutual collective responsibility for taxes began even earlier. The peasant could now sell his allotted land with some limitations. Some other legal disabilities were removed, and the Russian peasant doubtless became a freer individual than he was prior to 1905.

Central in this program, however, was the turnabout of the government with respect to mir tenure, which it had zealously guarded during the preceding half century. The new policy was not supported by many conservatives, who feared the sharp break with the paternalistic tradition, and it had a highly unfavorable reception among the liberal and radical opposition, including even those who were critical of the mir. It was felt that the government's antimir policy was too precipitate, too arbitrary, and, above all, sharply slanted in favor of a minority of the peasantry as against the great majority. Paul Miliukov sums up the opposition attitude thus:

> The Stolypin reform tried to divert peasants from the division of the land of the nobles by the division of their own land for the benefit of the most prosperous part of the peasantry.

Lenin, by the way, did not share this sentiment, common to the liberal and radical opposition. He wrote in 1912:

> Most reactionary are those Kadets from the [newspapers] *Rech'* and *Russkie vedomosti,* who reproach Stolypin for the breakup [of the mir] instead of demonstrating the necessity of a more consistent and decisive breakup.

The peasant reaction to the legislation may be gauged from the fact that out of more than nine million peasant households with communal land tenure in European Russia, about three million shifted voluntarily or involuntarily to hereditary tenure during the decade before the revolution of 1917. Thus, despite all blandishments and pressure, a majority of the peasants were still clinging to mir tenure on the eve of the revolution.

Whether this phase of Stolypin's policy contributed materially to agricultural progress, of which there was some after the revolution of 1905, is a debatable question. But this should not obscure the fact that other government measures, such as those leading to consolidation and segregation of fragmented peasant holdings, were clearly beneficial. Apart from any positive government action, however, the revolutionary storm and the freer climate after 1905, despite the reactionary character of the postrevolutionary political regime, doubtless had an energizing effect on the village. The vigorous growth during this period of the rural voluntary cooperative movement was a significant manifestation of the new spirit of grass-roots initiative.

Even in the matter of land, though the revolutionary disturbances of 1905 were suppressed and peasant aspirations for a new partition thwarted, many landowners became insecure and anxious to liquidate their estate properties at a good price. Thus, the acquisition of estate land by peasants through purchasing from landlords, which began soon after the emancipation, gathered momentum after 1905. It was assisted by the much expanded financial aid of a special government institution — the Peasant Bank. To be sure, a smaller area was involved and a stiffer price was exacted than would have been the case under the proposed liberal land-reform schemes of 1906–1907. Furthermore, the land often did not pass into the hands of those who needed it most. Be this as it may, about 30 per cent of the estate area was purchased by peasants between 1861 and the revolution of 1917. And on the eve of the revolution, small peasant farmers owned approximately two thirds of all land in European Russia outside of the public domain, which consisted mostly of nonagricultural land.

Peasant agriculture also extended eastward as the growing railroad network opened new agricultural areas for large-scale settlement beyond the Volga and the Urals. This colonization process, resembling in some respects the westward expansion of agriculture in the United States, was aided by the peasant disappointment produced by the abortive 1905 Revolution as well as by the lifting of various legal obstacles to mobility and by positive measures of government assistance. While speaking of the railroads, their effect in a country of vast distances in reducing the cultural and especially the economic self-sufficiency of the village and bringing it within the orbit of the market and money economy cannot be overestimated. Another important factor of change was the industrial revolution, which began in earnest during the closing decade of the nineteenth century. It expanded the domestic market for farm products and created new employment outlets for the underemployed rural manpower. Also the growth of the industrial working class, subject to strong radical propaganda by the intelligentsia, was bound to have political repercussions in the countryside, the more so since ties between the young Russian city proletariat and the village were far from sundered.

It seems legitimate to speculate that if a prolonged and exhausting war, culminating in a revolution and civil war, had not intervened in 1914–1918, agricultural improvement would have continued. If, in conjunction with such progress, the Stolypin policy of the "wager on the strong" could have been further implemented for a period of several decades, it is possible, though by no means certain, that the projected bulwark against an agrarian revolution might have been created. Again, it is probable that if a land reform could have been speedily enacted after the overthrow of the monarchy in 1917 by the democratic Provisional Government — and the difficulties of such an undertaking cannot be exaggerated — a peasant revolution might have been obviated. But all this was not to be.

Industrial Progress Was Improving the Economic System

ALEXANDER GERSHENKRON

Alexander Gershenkron is Professor of Economics and a member of the Russian Research Center at Harvard University. He is the author of several economic studies, the most recent being *Economic Backwardness in Historical Perspective* (1962). Deeply interested in the lessons of economic history that are applicable to present-day modernization in the underdeveloped nations, he has also spent many years studying Russian and Soviet economic development. In the selection below he presents his profound and valuable theory of the industrialization process and describes its unique development in Russia before 1917.

ECONOMIC development in a backward country such as Russia can be viewed as a series of attempts to find — or to create — substitutes for those factors which in more advanced countries had substantially facilitated economic development, but were lacking in conditions of Russian backwardness. Such "substitutions" are the key to an understanding of the way in which the original disabilities were overcome and a process of sustained industrial growth was started in Russia. It is these acts of substitution that came to determine the specific pattern of industrial development.

But the process of industrialization is also a process of diminishing backwardness. In its course, factors that were lacking formerly tend to become evident and acquire increasing importance within the body economic. What was once in vain looked for to serve as a "prerequisite" or a "cause" of industrial development came into being as its effect. It is a fascinating pursuit in the history of modern industrializations to see to what extent the original "substitutes" were thereby rendered obsolete and disappeared after having fulfilled their function; and to what extent they were preserved and continued to dominate the pattern of industrial development in its subsequent stages, even though the special need for them no longer existed. . . .

The great spurt of Russian industrialization in the prerevolutionary period largely coincided with the decade of the 1890's. Thus, almost thirty years had passed over the land before the great effort could come about. This is not surprising. The peasant reform would have had to be very different if a direct and immediate impact upon industrial growth could have been expected from it. Moreover, even if the reform had been deliberately designed to favor industrialization rather than to obstruct it, a certain preparatory period of slow growth was almost inevitable. The judicial and administrative reforms which came in the wake of the emancipation were essential in creating a framework for modern business activity. But other changes, at least equally significant, were much slower in coming. Certainly a radical improvement in communications was crucial. One does not have to conjure up the dramatic and pathetic vision of a huge boiler being dragged by teams of oxen through the deep mud of the Ukrainian steppes on its way to the construction site of the first blast furnace in the *Donbas* in order to understand that some railroad building had to antedate the period of rapid industrialization. Railroads were indispensable to sustain a level of exports consonant with the needs of an industrializing economy. Railroad materials had to be imported from abroad, which in turn meant pursuit of a liberal foreign-trade policy with but a modicum of encouragement to domestic industry. Besides, a period of rapid growth does not materialize overnight simply because an institutional barrier to industrialization has disappeared. Such a period requires a simultaneous development of complementary efforts in many directions. The component elements of growth in the individual industrial branches must be adjusted to each other, and only when a number of such "development blocks," to use Erik Dahmén's felicitous phrase, has been created is the stage set for the initiation of the great spurt.

There is little doubt that the decades following the emancipation can be conceived as such a period of preparation. And yet it is only in retrospect that they can be so viewed. The deficiency of the internal market, so untiringly stressed by the Populist writers, might have postponed the period of rapid growth until a far and indefinite future. The strategic factor in the great industrial upsurge of the 1890's must be seen in the changed policy of the government. The fear of industrialization, so much in evidence in the 1860's, was gone. Industrial development became an accepted and in fact the central goal. Once this happened, the problem of the peasant demand lost its previous significance, and its relation to industrialization was thoroughly reversed. It was as though a rotating stage had moved, revealing an entirely new scenery. The growth of peasant demand for industrial goods no longer was a prerequisite of successful industrialization. On the contrary, its curtailment became the objective. To reduce peasant consumption meant increasing the share of national output available for investment. It meant increased exports, stability of the currency, chances for larger and cheaper loans from abroad, and the availability of foreign exchange needed to service foreign loans.

The Russian state under Vyshnegradsky and Witte put the peasantry under very considerable fiscal pressure. It left the agricultural economy of the country to its own devices, satisfied that conversion of pastures into grain lands and some modest rise in productivity on those estates which were cultivated as such rather than leased to the peasants were sufficient to support the process of industrialization. Population of course was growing rapidly. In the closing years of the 1890's Russian agriculture produced less breadgrains per capita of the population than had been the case three decades earlier. If the increased exports are taken into consideration, the domestic availabilities were still smaller. A central principle of governmental policy was to impound a larger share of the peasants' output rather than to take active steps to raise that output.

Thus, the government's budgetary policy was effectively *substituted* for the deficiency of an internal market. The continuation of railroad construction on a large scale throughout the 1890's provided the government with convenient machinery for the maintenance of demand for industrial products. At the same time, in multifarious ways the government either supplied investment funds to industry directly or encouraged and facilitated investment in industry. Government action took the place of what in other countries was achieved by the pull of a growing free market, or by forced savings generated either by credit creation or by the impact upon current income of previously accumulated claims.

Those, however, were not the only processes of substitution that were taking place during the period of the great spurt of Russian industrialization. The Russian government, far from favoring all branches of industrial endeavor indiscriminately, concentrated its primary attention on the output of iron and steel and the machinery industries. The strategic interest in railroads and general political considerations certainly prompted the government in that direction. But as may be deduced from comparisons with other countries, this cannot be more than a part of the story. In a sense, this concentration upon certain branches of industry also was an emanation of substitutive processes.

Russia on the eve of its great industrial spurt suffered from many disabilities. Its entrepreneurs were far too few; their time horizon often limited, their commercial customs backward, and their standards of honesty none too high. The influx of labor to industry was inadequate because of the institutional framework that had been imposed upon agriculture. Such labor as was available was uneducated, restless and fitful in its habits, often trying to submerge the sense of frustration and loneliness in alcoholic excesses with consequent absenteeism, low productivity, and rebellion against the rules of the factory discipline. One of the few advantages that Russia, as many other backward countries in similar conditions, possessed was the possibility of borrowing technology from more advanced and more experienced industrial countries. In this field alone, Russia could equal, if not excel, them. It could concentrate on modern technology so that its factory equipment, though much smaller in the aggregate, could be much more up-to-date in its average composition. But the introduction on a large scale of technology from advanced countries, in its very nature, also meant a substitution of capital for labor. Far from being irrational in conditions of a backward country, it was the modern Western technology which enabled the Russian entrepreneurs to overcome the disability of an inadequate labor supply and very frequently also the inferior quality of that labor.

This is not to say that lack of suitable industrial labor in itself was not a hindrance to Russian industrialization. Introduction of a labor-saving process may mean lower cost per unit of the product; and still the entrepreneur may find the resulting saving insufficient to justify the effort of reorganization and modernization of the plant. His decision may be positive only if he feels that cost reductions will lead to a great expansion of output, thus increasing the total profits very considerably. But a sizable expansion of output, even though the innovation is labor saving, will require a large increase in the labor force; accordingly, the decision may still fall against the innovation, unless the labor needed may be expected to come forth without too great a rise in wage rates. The point, therefore, is not that the difficulties which Russia experienced with the formation of an industrial proletariat were not a bothersome obstacle. The point rather is that the assurance of government demand for a considerable portion of the growing output in conjunction with the introduction of modern technology created a situation in which the quantitative and the qualitative inadequacy of the labor supply could be neutralized to an extent that still permitted a relatively high rate of industrial growth.

A historian of the period cannot fail to be impressed with two aspects of this process of assimilation of foreign technology. It may be taken for granted that throughout the nineteenth century technology tended to become more and more labor saving. This was true of the individual industrial branches, and even more so of industrial economies as a whole, because of the increasing share of those industries where technological progress led to particularly rapid increases in the capital-labor ratios. It is true of course that, broadly speaking, the Russian entrepreneurs had to accept Western technology such as it was. But if they had wanted to keep down the capital-labor ratios, they might well have tried to obtain secondhand equipment built in earlier phases of Western industrialization. The least they could do was to try to import technology from those countries where technological progress had been less rapid. In fact, the opposite was true. In the period of the great spurt of the nineties, it was no longer the English technology, but the more progressive German technology that came to dominate Russian imports; and increasingly, the eyes of engineers and factory managers turned toward the United States whence even more capital-intensive equipment was brought into the country. Thus alternatives were available, and there is no reason to assume that the choices made were not the rational ones.

On the other hand, it would be wrong to see the process of technological acquisition as one of mere imitation. True, in the last decade of the nineteenth century, the Russians had as yet very little opportunity for producing equipment which combined certain features of, say, American and German machinery (as began to happen several decades later). But they exercised discretion in the processes that were modernized and those that were left unchanged, often within the same plant. While the Russian blast furnaces were rapidly becoming bigger and technically more advanced, the processes of introducing the charge into the furnaces remained untouched by this development, and workers equipped with wheelbarrows still carried out the job. Where industrial work was still similar to that used in agriculture and capable of being performed by an unskilled and fluctuating labor force, it was allowed to continue to do so.

Finally, there is the problem of bigness. Bigness, in a broad sense, is of course inherent in the concept of a great spurt. But the industrialization in Russia, as in so many other backward countries in the nineteenth century, was also characterized by bigness both of individual plant and individual enterprise. There were many reasons for this. For one, the technology of the nineteenth century typically favored the large plants, and to accept the most advanced technology also meant accepting larger and larger plants. The state promoting industrial establishments, for good and not so good reasons, showed remarkably little interest in small businesses. Large enterprises were a much more lucrative source of graft; and the corruption of the bureaucracy tended to reinforce a tendency that was already present for weighty economic reasons. Similarly, the Russian government did little to check the strong cartelization movement within Russian industry which acquired momentum after the great spurt of the nineties. But what is of interest here is that the bigness of plant and enterprise, too, must be viewed as a specific substitution process. The lack of managerial and entrepreneurial personnel was compensated for by a scale of plants which made it possible to spread the thin layer of available talent over a large part of the industrial economy.

But what were the results and the aftermath of these developments? In purely quantitative terms, in terms of growth of industrial output, the spurt was truly a great one. The average annual rate of industrial growth during the nineties was around 8 per cent, and it was even better than that in the last years of the decade. None of the major countries in Western Europe had experienced a comparably high rate of change. The very rapidity of the transformation, however, was making for maladjustments of various kinds. The discrepancy between the industrial segment of the economy which was forging ahead and the relatively stagnant agricultural segment perhaps was the most crucial among those lags and tensions. But others were by no means unimportant.

The specific processes of substitution, which have been referred to above, tended to reinforce the heterogeneous character of the resulting economic structure. Contrasts between the new and the old appeared within the industrial group itself and within the individual plants and enterprises. Technology as a strategic factor in the industrial spurt implied modernization of some industrial branches and not of others. Within an industrial plant age-old processes based on tools used in the construction of the Pyramids were carried on side by side with methods representing the last word of the inventive genius of the nineteenth century. This inevitably was reflected in human contrasts within the labor force.

But the contrasts obviously transcended labor; they extended into the managerial group. The technical director, as the chief engineer frequently was called in a Russian factory, may have been indistinguishable from his Western counterpart. The commercial manager or the entrepreneur as likely as not was a much more complex phenomenon. He was able to understand and willing to exploit the economic advantages of the new technology, but at the same time he carried on attitudes and displayed forms of behavior which differed little, if at all, from those of preindustrial entrepreneurs in Russia. This was true of his relations to consumers, suppliers, credit institutions, and competitors. In addition, his relations with the governmental bureaucracy called for special, often very devious, actions. He had to be a different man in his way of dealing with a German firm which supplied his business firm with machinery and know-how, and in dealing with an official in the Ministry of Finance whence he obtained both subsidies and orders for deliveries. The great spurt in conditions of Russian backwardness could not fail to give rise to manifold stresses, tensions, and incongruities. Sociological research which would view those tensions against the economic background of the mechanics of backwardness should discover a rich field for empirical findings and analytical comprehension.

All these disparities, created almost inevitably in the course of the great spurt, can be seen as problems for the succeeding phase of Russian industrial development that followed. However, overriding all of them in importance was the problem which the emancipation of the peasantry did not solve and the gravity of which was greatly enhanced precisely by the policy of rapid industrialization. Industrialization required political stability, but industrialization, the cost of which was largely defrayed by the peasantry, was in itself a threat to political stability and hence to the continuation of the policy of industrialization. The immediate effect of the basic substitution of the government's budgetary policies for the deficiency of the internal market was growth of industrial output. In the longer run, the effects were more complex.

What happened in Russia in the nineties of the last century was the great upsurge of modern industrialization. Nevertheless, certain aspects of it were not modern at all. Several times before in the course of Russian history, economic development seemed to follow a curious pattern: the military interests of the state induced the government to bring about a rapid spurt of economic growth. In the course of the process, heavy burdens were imposed upon the peasant population of the country, the enserfment of the Russian peasantry having been inextricably connected with the policies of economic development. So great were the burdens, and so heavy the pressure, that after a number of years the spurt tended to peter out, leaving an exhausted population to recover slowly from the stress and the strain that had been imposed upon it.

There is little doubt that military considerations had a good deal to do with the Russian government's conversion to a policy of rapid industrialization. True, no immediate military discomfiture preceded the initiation of the new policy. But the war of 1877 against the Turks was won on the battlefields in the Danube Valley and the Balkan Mountains, only to be lost in Berlin against the British and probably the Germans as well. In the course of the Berlin congress, particularly during its dramatic moments, the Russian government had much opportunity and reason to reflect that it was not much better prepared for any military conflict with a Western power than it had been a quarter of a century earlier on the eve of the Crimean War. In the short run, Russian reaction consisted in shifting the direction of its expansionist policy away from Europe to Central Asia and the Far East. Taking a somewhat longer view and further prompted by the formation of military alliances in Central Europe, the government turned toward the goal of a drastic increase in the economic potential of the country.

In the 1890's, a renewed enserfment of the peasantry was, of course, not in the realm of practical politics. Nor was there any need for such a measure. The reforms of rural administration which had been introduced with the advent of reaction under Alexander III gave the central bureaucracy sufficient tax-exacting power over the peasantry; at least for some time it was possible to keep the peasantry in the state of docile compliance. The joint responsibility of the village commune for tax payments was helpful, though far from indispensable. The considerable shift to indirect taxation further increased the government's ability to pay for the industrialization in conditions of a relative price and currency stability. The fiscal policy of the government was able to perform the function which at an earlier age had been performed by the institution of serfdom.

The great spurt of the 1890's came to an end in 1900. The depression of that year was variously interpreted as an overproduction crisis, a financial crash, or a response to economic setbacks abroad, particularly in Central Europe. It is fairly clear, however, that below the surface phenomena lay the exhaustion of the tax-paying powers of the rural population. The patience of the peasantry was at its end. The following years were characterized by growing unrest in the villages until the folly of the war with Japan fanned the isolated fires into the flame of a widespread peasant rebellion in the course of the 1905 Revolution. All this was very much like the consummation of the traditional pattern of Russian economic development: a quick upsurge compressed within a relatively short period ending in years of stagnation. And yet there was a great deal more to the industrial spurt of the 1890's than simply a repetition of previous sequences of economic development. It would seem more plausible to view those similarities as the last emanations, in prerevolutionary Russia, of the traditional pattern. For the differences were fully as important as the similarities. Also in this broad sense, the new and the old appeared curiously commingled. Along with the resurrection of a specifically Russian past, there was also the assimilation of Russian economic development into a graduated but still general pattern of European industrialization.

Two, and perhaps three, factors stand out in distinguishing the upswing of the

1890's from similar episodes in the more remote past. One of them has just been mentioned. During the decade of the 1890's, the Russian government abstained from introducing for the sake of the industrialization any far-reaching institutional change which, while aiding the process in the short run, would have become a serious obstacle to its continuation in the long run. Neither the institution of the *zemskii nachal'nik* nor the additional steps taken in the 1890's to preserve and protect the village commune could of course compare in any way with the enserfment of the peasantry. That a government firmly committed to the policy of industrialization went out of its way to safeguard the obshchina seemed paradoxical. But apart from the fiscal value of the arrangement, it was felt that its existence contributed to political stability within the country. Neither reason was persuasive. Satisfactory substitutes for joint responsibility for tax payments could easily have been found; and the events of the subsequent years showed clearly that the village commune nursed rebellious rather than conservative sentiments. The abolition of the commune still remained a problem of industrial policies in Russia, but it was one which antedated the period of rapid industrialization.

The other factor was positive. A modern industrialization based on the creation of fixed capital of considerable durability was not followed by periods of protracted stagnations as easily as had been the earlier, much more labor-intensive spurts of economic development ("stagnation" of course is to be understood simply in terms of a very low or even negative rate of growth). The recuperative power of a capital-intensive economy was greatly superior to that of its historical predecessors. And, finally, a modern industrialization is characterized also by a more substantial investment in human capital. In particular, it tends to bring about, over a relatively short period, a considerable change in entrepreneurial and managerial attitudes as well as, though to a lesser extent, in those of skilled labor. All this means that the effects of the great spurt reached out strongly into the future; that the process of industrialization could be resumed at diminished *faux frais* and in a form more efficient and less dependent upon the support of the state.

Such were the characteristic features of Russian industrial growth in the years between the 1905 Revolution and the outbreak of World War I. This, too, was a period of rather rapid growth (some 6 per cent per year), even though the rate of change remained below that of the 1890's. During those years industrialization could no longer be the primary concern of the government. War and revolution had greatly strained budgetary capabilities. The redemption payments (as well as the institution of joint responsibility) had disappeared under the impact of the revolution. Kokovtsev, first as Minister of Finance and later as head of the Cabinet, pursued a cautious policy of thrift. Railroad building continued, but on a much reduced scale. The execution of such armament plans as were conceived was being postponed from year to year. In the eighteenth century, the death of Peter the Great and the withdrawal of the state from active economic policy spelled the doom of the contemporaneous economic development. But in Russia of the twentieth century, Count Witte's fall and the abandonment of his policies did not prevent a renewed outburst of industrial activity.

Nothing underscores more clearly the changed attitude of the government than the fact that its most important action in the field of economic policy was Stolypin's legislation against the obshchina. In a radical reversal of the agrarian policies pursued only a few years earlier, Stolypin's reforms of 1906 and 1910 made it possible for the peasants to sever their connection with the obshchina through a simple and advantageous procedure, to acquire personal ownership of the land, and in the process often to swap the numerous strips of their former allotment for a single consolidated holding.

There is no question that many aspects of the reform were harsh and unfair to the less prosperous members of the village communes. There is also every evidence that the government's *volte-face* was caused by political considerations, that is to say, by the impressive lesson learned from peasant uprisings during the preceding revolution. The consequences of the reform for the process of industrial development were accidental from the government's point of view, despite some liberal phraseology ("liberal" in the European sense of the term) used in defending the reforms.

Nevertheless, the potential positive effects of the reform on industrial development were indisputable. The authors of the reform, despite considerable opposition within the government, refused to accept the concept of family or household ownership; the ownership of peasants leaving the village commune was vested in the head of the household. For the first time, the road was open for an unimpaired movement to the city of peasant family members; for the first time large groups of Russian peasants could, like their counterparts in the West, sell the land and use the proceeds for establishing themselves outside agriculture. The war of 1914 necessarily cut short the implementation of the reform, but its initial effect was considerable. Both those peasants who had felt that leaving the commune would enable them to increase the productivity of their farms and those peasants who had been anxious to leave the village hastened to avail themselves of the separation procedure. It was a considerable step on the road of Russia's westernization.

And this is the aspect of the reform that is of primary importance from the point of view of the present discussion. The economic stagnation that followed the reign of Peter the Great was burdened by the legacy of serfdom. The very modernization of the state machinery under Peter meant that the government was much better equipped to enforce the serfdom condition upon the peasantry and to deal effectively with fugitives from serf status. At the same time, the territorial expansion of Russia kept reducing and making more remote the frontier regions which formerly had been the sanctuary of so many peasants in their flight from oppression. It was under these conditions that the edict granting the nobility and the gentry freedom from service obligations marked the acme of the state's retirement from active guidance of the country's economic life. That act finally severed the original connection between serfdom and economic development and sealed the perpetuation of serfdom as a main obstacle to economic progress. With regard to both its historical locus and its "liberalizing" character, the Imperial Edict of Peter III (1762) bears a certain resemblance to Stolypin's reform. And yet, despite these similarities, it is the difference between the two measures which may be taken as a gauge of the contrast in historical situations. The great spurt under Peter the Great had not led to sustained growth. The traditional pattern of Russian economic development was allowed to work itself out fully. By contrast, the withdrawal of the state after the upswing of the 1890's was marked by a measure which was designed to further rather than thwart industrial progress.

The westernization of Russian industrialization between 1906 and 1914 expressed itself in a large variety of ways. To use the previously adopted terminology, one could say that the pattern of substitutions was changing rapidly. To some extent banks stepped into the vacuum left by the state. In this way, credit-creation policies and some entrepreneurial guidance by the banks continued to substitute for the scarcity of both capital and entrepreneurship in Russia. But this mode of substitution tended to approximate the pattern of Russian development to that prevailing in Central Europe. The credit policies of the banks were still a substitute for an autonomous internal market, but there is little doubt that one of the consequences of the industrial creations of the nineties was the gradual emergence of such a market.

It may be quite tempting to view again

the change between the period under review and that of the 1890's in terms of Erik Dahmén's dichotomy between development blocks in the state of full completion and development blocks in the beginning stage. The years 1906–1914 were characterized by the relative scarcities of coal, oil, and metals, in conjunction with the rapid forging ahead of metal-processing industries. There is a persistent and very much exaggerated tendency in present Russian historiography to present those scarcities as consequences of monopolistic policies in the basic-materials industries. It is probably more reasonable, still following Dahmén, to say that during the years preceding the First World War the structure of Russian industry was distinguished by specific disproportionalities and that once again, though on a much higher level, industry may have been passing through a period of dynamic preparation for another great spurt. Such a spurt, of course, never materialized. The point, however, is that considering the years 1906–1914 as a period of formation of new development blocks may help to explain why the rate of growth during those years was not higher than it was. It cannot explain the high growth that was actually attained in a situation where the outside aid to industry had manifestly declined to a fraction of its previous volume. It is more helpful, therefore, to regard this period as governed by the effects of diminished backwardness, and in this sense to view the whole stretch between the end of the 1880's and the outbreak of the war as consisting of two disparate and yet connected parts: the great spurt of the 1890's had prepared for the subsequent continuation of growth under changed conditions.

Many of the tensions and frictions that could be so strikingly observed during the 1890's reappeared in the second period, if at all, in a considerably modified and tempered form. There is no question that great progress had taken place with regard to entrepreneurial attitudes. Without such progress and, in particular, without the general rise in trustworthiness of Russian businessmen, the banks could never have come to play a powerful role as suppliers of long-term credit to industrial firms. The general modernization of entrepreneurial attitudes no doubt made the complex of actions and relations of the individual entrepreneurs less heterogeneous. The decline in the importance of the government as an economic agent pointed in the same direction.

The years that had passed since the second half of the 1880's considerably increased the stock of permanent industrial labor in the country. At the same time, after 1905, more tangible improvements both in real wages and in working conditions became noticeable. The reduction in the importance of foreign engineers and foremen in factories and mines also tended to diminish friction. At the same time, the great pressure upon the peasantry had subsided. In contrast to the last decades of the nineteenth century, the quantity of breadgrain available for domestic consumption rose faster than did the population. The industrialization between 1906 and 1914 no longer offers a picture of a race against time and of progressive exhaustion, physically and mentally, of the population's power to suffer and to endure. . . . One might surmise that in the absence of the war Russia would have continued on the road of progressive westernization.

It is not entirely pointless to speculate on what might have happened in the course of such a development. Diminution of backwardness is a complex process. As has already been noted, certain paraphernalia of backwardness are shed fairly soon after the beginning of the process. Other elements are more resistant to change. Thus, the great school of industrialization tends to educate the entrepreneurs before it educates the workers; and it takes still longer before the influence of the industrial sector of the economy penetrates into the countryside and begins to affect the attitudes of the peasantry. In the latter respect, prerevolutionary Russia saw no more than the first modest traces of such an influence. Yet the likelihood that the transformation in agriculture would have gone on at an accelerated speed is very great. . . .

The only purpose in speculating about the probable course of Russian economic development as it might have been, if not interrupted by war and revolution, is to try to cast more light on the general industrial trends that dominated the last period of industrialization in prerevolutionary Russia. Still the question remains whether war and revolution cannot be interpreted as the result of the preceding industrial development. Some Soviet historians certainly incline in that direction. If the Russian bourgeoisie could be saddled with the main responsibility for the outbreak of the war and if, in addition, it could be shown that in bringing about the war it had acted in response to the pressure of its economic interests — if, in short, the process of Russian industrialization carried in itself the seeds of the coming military conflict — then to abstract the war from the process in order to elucidate the course and prospects of Russian industrialization would mean to abstract the process as well. Some Russian manufacturers indeed may have welcomed the wartime orders for their products. Yet the precise mechanism through which such interests of the bourgeoisie were in fact translated into the decisions reached by the emperor and his government has remained altogether obscure.

The view just described seems to magnify the political significance of the Russian bourgeoisie out of all proportion and to substitute suppositions of various degrees of plausibility for historical evidence. It might be more persuasive to argue that the government saw a relatively short and victorious war as a chance to solidify the regime and to avert the danger of revolution. And the question then would be to what extent the preceding industrial development may be said to have been leading to another revolutionary cataclysm.

It is true, of course, that the social and political structure of the empire was shot through with manifold serious weaknesses. Opposition to the regime was nearly universal among the intelligentsia and certainly widespread among the industrial and mercantile groups. Since 1912, the year of the famous massacre in the Lena gold fields, the strike movement of the workers was again gaining momentum. And at the bottom of the social edifice there was the old resentment of the peasants who had never accepted the rightfulness of the gentry's ownership rights over the land. The peasantry's land hunger was a steady source of ferment. The sentiment in the villages was no doubt further exacerbated by the blows struck against the village commune and the threat of its dissolution. A new outbreak of revolutionary violence at some point was far from being altogether improbable.

And yet, as one compares the situation in the years before 1914 with that of the nineties, striking differences are obvious. In the earlier period, the very process of industrialization with its powerful confiscatory pressures upon the peasantry kept adding, year in and year out, to the feelings of resentment and discontent until the outbreak of large-scale disorders became almost inevitable. The industrial prosperity of the following period had no comparable effects, however. Modest as the improvements in the situation of peasants were, they were undeniable and widely diffused. Those improvements followed rather than preceded a revolution and accordingly tended to contribute to a relaxation of tension. Stolypin's reforms certainly were an irritant, but after the initial upsurge their implementation was bound to proceed in a much more gradual fashion.

Similarly, the economic position of labor was clearly improving. In the resurgence of the strike movement economic problems seemed to predominate. It is true, of course, that in the specific conditions of the period any wage conflict tended to assume a political character because of the ready interventions of police and military forces on behalf of management. But this did not mean that the climate of opinion and emotion within the labor movement was becoming more revolutionary; as shown by the history of European countries (such as Austria or Belgium), sharp political struggles marked the period of formation of labor movements that in actual fact, though not always in the language used, were committed to reformism. There is little doubt that the Russian labor movement of those years was slowly turning toward revision and trade-unionist lines. As was true in the West, the struggles for general and equal franchise to the Duma and for a cabinet responsible to the Duma, which probably would have occurred sooner or later, may well have further accentuated this development. To repeat, I do not mean to deny that there was much political instability in the country. There clearly was. What matters here is that from the point of view of the industrial development of the country, war, revolution, or the threat thereof may reasonably be seen as extraneous phenomena. In this sense, it seems plausible to say that Russia on the eve of the war was well on the way toward a westernization or, perhaps more precisely, a Germanization of its industrial growth. The "old" in the Russian economic system was definitely giving way to the "new." . . .

Modernization Was Making Revolution More Remote

MICHAEL KARPOVICH

THE DUMA AND THE GOVERNMENT

The political order established in Russia after the revolution of 1905 has often been described as "sham-constitutionalism," and the Duma has been disparaged as a mere "smoke-screen for autocracy" or a "convenient tool in the hands of the government." For the prevalence of this idea the representatives of the Russian opposition must be held largely responsible. In the heat of their struggle for a real parliamentary government it was natural for them to emphasize and even to exaggerate the many limitations from which the work of the Duma had to suffer. To a historian, however, the period appears in a somewhat different light. Even if there was no parliament in Russia, there certainly was a constitutional régime. And although the tsar retained his historical title of autocrat, this was rather a mere verbal concession to the centuries-old tradition and a glaring anachronism. In reality his power was no longer absolute because it was limited by the Fundamental Laws, which provided for the obligatory concurrence of the Duma in legislation. Strictly speaking, the Russian autocracy ceased to exist with the publication of the manifesto of October 17, 1905.

Of course, it must be admitted that the Duma, as finally established, was not a real parliament in the modern European sense of the word. To begin with, it did not represent the whole people, being based on a limited and unequal franchise which favored the large landowners and the city bourgeoisie to the detriment of the lower classes. National minorities also were discriminated against as compared with the purely Russian element of the population. Equally important were the limitations imposed upon the powers of the Duma. Under the Fundamental Laws, which could be changed only upon the initiative of the crown, the emperor enjoyed the exclusive right of directing foreign policy and the complete control of the executive. The ministers were responsible to him only and all the appointments both in the army and in the civil service were made in his name and required no further confirmation. Parts of the budget were declared to be "iron-clad," that is exempt from examination by the Duma. Article 87 of the Fundamental Laws reserved for the government the right to promulgate emergency legislation, in the intervals between the Duma sessions, by means of imperial decrees. This proved to be a convenient device to pass those measures which would meet with strong opposition. Although such laws had to be subsequently submitted to the Duma for ratification the latter, confronted in each case with an accomplished fact, usually found its freedom of action greatly hindered. Finally, to create one more check upon the activities of the Duma, the old bureaucratic Council of State was transformed into an upper chamber and its consent was made requisite for the passage of bills into laws. As only one half of its membership was elected, and that from public bodies representative of the upper groups of Russian society, while the other half was appointed by the crown, the Council of State could be counted upon to offer effective resistance should the Duma display an undesirable zeal for reform.

Yet one cannot discard the Duma as a negligible factor in Russian political life after 1907. Of great importance was the very fact that the principle of self-government now was extended to the field of national administration, from which heretofore it had been so consistently excluded. Moreover, in spite of all the above-mentioned limitations, the Duma still was able to exercise a real influence upon the conduct of national affairs. Although, as we have seen, it was not an adequate representation of the Russian people, it nevertheless could voice the demands of independent public elements and from its tribune governmental policies could be subjected by the opposition to an outspoken criticism not subject to censorship and receiving the widest publicity possible. Nor was the Duma entirely powerless in its relations with the executive. It still retained the right to examine and vote upon the greater part of the budget, and consequently every minister who desired to pass his estimates through the Duma was somewhat bound to seek its good will. The other weapon in the hands of the legislative chamber was its right of interpellation, that is, of asking explanations from the heads of the executive departments. And although, even in case of a unanimous censure, nothing happened to the minister in question so long as he retained the confidence of his sovereign, the Russian bureaucrats did not remain entirely insensitive to the attitude of popular representatives. As a matter of fact, under the influence of the Duma many departments of the central government became notably modernized and liberalized.

Finally, during the few years of its peaceful existence the Duma was able to pass various legislative measures constituting in their entirety quite a creditable positive achievement. A scheme of universal education was introduced and appropriations were voted for a corresponding annual increase in the number of primary schools throughout the Empire. Measures were taken to endow the peasants with full civil rights, putting them on a basis of equality with other classes; the office of "land captain" was abolished and the jurisdiction of the justices of the peace was extended to country districts. The Zemstvo institutions were established in nine additional provinces, important labor legislation was passed, and a very substantial improvement was achieved in the field of national defense. To sum up, the Duma succeeded "in making itself an indispensable factor in the national life of Russia and in retaining, in spite of all the obstacles in its way, the vital essence inherent in the very principle of popular representation" (Miliukov).

The relations between the Duma and the government remained not very satisfactory even after the drastic change in the electoral law which assured the preponderance of moderate elements in the legislative chamber. The sponsor of this measure, Peter Stolypin, Prime Minister during 1906-11, hardly could be called a consistent constitutionalist, in the strict sense of the word, as he seldom hesitated to apply extra-constitutional methods whenever he thought it necessary. It must be admitted, however, that he sincerely valued the coöperation of the Duma in legislative activity and had no thought of going back to the old autocratic ways of governing Russia. A man of upright character and great ability, he was hailed by his admirers as "the Russian Bismarck" and denounced by the opposition as a high-handed reactionary. To-day it is possible to appraise him calmly and without exaggeration. That he was heart and soul in favor of Russia's progress seems to be certain; to call him a reactionary would be obviously unjust. His agrarian policy showed that he possessed both foresight and determination. But with all his outstanding qualities he lacked broad-mindedness and subtlety and thus fell short of becoming a really great statesman. In his methods he was often too dictatorial and he did not know how to manage men and parties. His end was tragic and in a way symbolical. In 1911 he was assassinated by an agent of the secret political police who at the same time was a member of a revolutionary organization. Only a few months before, Stolypin had himself defended in the Duma the use as *agents-provocateurs* of such double-dealing persons, seeing in it a necessary weapon in the government's war on the revolutionaries.

After Stolypin's death the governmental policy towards the Duma became more inconsistent and vacillating. To the end of the imperial régime there was no unified cabinet in Russia, each minister being directly responsible to the emperor, with the Prime Minister occupying a position of merely honorary chairmanship. The result was that while some of the members of the government were more or less liberally inclined and desired to coöperate with the Duma, others were undisguised reactionaries and did not hesitate to display their hostility toward popular representation. With the emperor ill-suited to the rôle of constitutional monarch and not always willing to play the part at all, the reactionaries were able at times to get the upper hand in governmental councils and to place some irritating obstacles in the way of the legislative assembly. It was as a result of this policy that the moderate wing of the Duma gradually began to shift its position to the left until the way was prepared for a political understanding between the Cadets, on the one hand, and the Octobrists and even some of the Nationalists, on the other. The alignment of Duma parties on the eve of the World War foreshadowed a new conflict between the constitutional opposition and the forces of reaction entrenched in the government. And of the two the opposition had a much better chance of success because it was supported by the general trend of Russia's social and intellectual evolution.

* * *

CULTURAL PROGRESS UNDER THE CONSTITUTIONAL RÉGIME

Not only the body but the soul of Russia as well was growing stronger and healthier during the decade which preceded the World War. Progress in the field of education was no less striking than that on the economic side. The most pressing problem was to reduce in the shortest time possible the appallingly high percentage of illiteracy which still prevailed within the country. The Duma, the government and the Zemstvos applied themselves to the task with an energy and a determination that were without precedent in Russian history. It was only in this period that elementary education in Russia was finally put on a firm basis. In 1908, when the scheme of universal education was first advanced as a practical proposition, there had been somewhat less than one hundred thousand primary schools in the country. By the end of 1913 this figure was increased to one hundred and fifty thousand and definite plans were worked out to establish during the following decade a number of new schools sufficient to take care of every child in the Empire. The realization of this plan was made more or less secure by correspondingly large appropriations: in 1914 the expenses for popular education showed an increase of 628 per cent over the budget of 1894.

In the secondary schools and the universities (of which there were now eleven as compared with six in the first half of the nineteenth century) the number of students had increased rapidly; at the same time these educational institutions were becoming more and more accessible to the lower classes. There was also notable progress as far as freedom of teaching was concerned. Even in the secondary schools political pressure on the part of the government became hardly noticeable. The universities which, since the publication of the new statute of 1905, had been governed by their own faculties on the basis of academic autonomy, enjoyed a practically complete freedom of teaching. There were still occasional sharp conflicts between the universities and the government, but these conflicts arose almost invariably out of the political activities of the students and had nothing to do with the character of instruction.

Generally speaking, the constitutional régime brought with it a very considerable relaxation of governmental censorship. To be sure, during the period of reaction which followed the revolution of 1905 the censor still remained very active, but if compared with the preceding period his efforts were neither so far-reaching nor so effective. The revolutionary events stimulated discussion of political and social subjects and this continued even after the suppression of the revolution. The daily press occupied now a much more important place in national life than ever before and the opposition newspapers were able, in spite of all the obstacles in their way, to present their views and to influence public opinion. A similar phenomenon of great importance was the progress of religious toleration. A law published in 1905 made religious affiliation a matter of free choice with every Russian citizen and gave the "old believers" and the sectarians a legal status, although still retaining the privileged position of the Greek Orthodox Church. In the ranks of the latter voices began to be heard in favor of liberating the church from governmental control; a significant movement started among the laity and the clergy aiming at the convocation of a church council and the reëstablishment of the Patriarchate.

One of the beneficial results of the constitutional reform was the emancipation of the intellectual life of educated Russia from the exclusive domination of politics. With the establishment of the Duma, the formation of legally recognized parties and the relaxation of censorship, a wider outlet was created for political energy and interest. This permitted the other fields of intellectual activity to regain their independence. Pure science, art for art's sake, and abstract philosophical thinking were reëstablished in a position of honor and ceased to be looked upon as mere reactionary devices, designed to divert public opinion from consideration of civic problems. The somewhat narrow and intolerant creed of the radical *intelligentsia* began to lose its unity and vitality. Intellectual life became more diversified; new and highly interesting tendencies were manifesting themselves both in literature and in art. A poetical renaissance took place with the appearance in Russia of the symbolist school, which exercised also a considerable influence on the Russian novel and drama. Literary criticism was divorced from political and social propaganda; a complete revision of literary values was undertaken from a purely artistic point of view. There was a similar development in Russian painting, which became more concerned with the quest for beauty and less willing to serve any purpose other than its own.

Among those who still remained true to the ideal of civic duty there were also noticeable some significant changes. It looked as if the professional revolutionary, with his peculiar psychology shaped by underground activities, was rapidly becoming a thing of the past. In place of a self-appointed savior of humanity, a type to which so many of the old intellectuals belonged, there was now appearing the expert, ready to apply his special knowledge wherever it was needed. The whole relationship between the *intelligentsia* and the popular masses was gradually assuming a more normal character. On the part of the intellectuals there was less of a somewhat morbid desire to atone for the sins of their fathers by a self-denying ministry to the "people," while the masses themselves were just beginning to lose their deep-seated distrust of the educated man as a member of the privileged minority. The formation of a new layer of the *intelligentsia,* actually coming from the lower classes, promised to play a most important part in this connection. This development was only in its early stages; there still remained a dangerously wide gulf separating the educated class of Russia from the majority of the nation.

* * *

CONCLUSION

Imperial Russia is now a thing of the past. An historian should attempt to view it in its entirety and to approach it with necessary detachment. Its record is not one of unmitigated evil; it has to its credit many outstanding positive achievements. Moreover, at the time of its fall it was by no means beyond the hope of regeneration. During the period which forms the subject of this study the Russian imperial régime did not remain unchanged but on the contrary was undergoing a process of constant modification. Reforms usually came too late and, as a rule, were followed by periods of reaction, but on the whole it was a forward movement, not a retrogression. On the eve of the World War Russia was profoundly different from what she had been in the beginning of the nineteenth century. In spite of the deadweight of the past and the acute contradictions of the present, it was a steadily and rapidly progressing country. In view of this progress it would be hardly correct to assert that the revolution was absolutely inevitable. Russia still had to solve many complicated and difficult problems but the possibility of their peaceful solution was by no means excluded. To the extent that the country was growing economically more prosperous and culturally more advanced, this possibility was constantly gaining strength and the danger of a violent upheaval was becoming more remote.

To this hope of peaceful evolution the war dealt a staggering blow. It caught Russia in the very process of radical internal reorganization. The constitutional experiment was less than a decade old; the agrarian legislation of Stolypin had been in operation for a few years only; the scheme of universal education was just beginning to be realized; the industrial development, rapid as it was, had not yet passed beyond its early stages. Under such conditions the war was bound to produce grave disturbances in the internal life of the country. A heroic and concerted effort on the part of the whole nation was needed if the imperial structure was to weather the storm. To such an indispensable effort, the political crisis of 1915-1917 was an insurmountable obstacle. The war made the revolution highly probable, but human folly made it inevitable.

UNSOLVED PROBLEMS

No Political Alternative to Autocracy Had Adequate Support

CYRIL E. BLACK

Cyril E. Black, Professor of History at Princeton University, is one of America's leading proponents of the theory of modernization. Author and editor of numerous works on East European and Russian history, his most valuable contributions to the study of modernization in Russia are *The Transformation of Russian Society* (1960), which he edited and to which he contributed an "Introduction" and a "Conclusion," and the *Slavic Review* article from which the following excerpts have been taken. In this selection, he makes the very significant point that while modernization was well along by 1917, Russia had not yet developed any political alternative to the autocracy with sufficient support to enable it to ride through the crises of that year.

I

THE modern revolution was intellectual in its origins, resting as it did on the phenomenal expansion of knowledge which had its roots in the Middle Ages, and its initial impact on Russia was similarly intellectual. This impact may be traced back to the movements favoring the revision of religious texts and doctrine in the fifteenth and sixteenth centuries, and to the appearance in the seventeenth century of isolated nobles with a Western outlook. It was nevertheless not until the eighteenth century that there was a general turning to the West on the part of the state and the nobility, and only in the nineteenth century did the problem of "Russia and Europe" come to absorb the full attention of Russian intellectuals. The diversity and brilliance of Russian political and literary thought concerning the relationship of traditional to modern values and institutions is probably matched only by that of China and Japan among non-European peoples. It produced a wide spectrum of interpretations, ranging from the strongest reaffirmation of the rightness and sanctity of the Russian way of doing things to the view that the imperial state was a form of "oriental despotism" which must be destroyed to make way for the socialist society toward which mankind was alleged to be moving ineluctably.

This rich body of thought moved in two currents, which were continually intermingling but which remained reasonably distinct. The first was represented by the political leaders and high officials, starting with Peter the Great and ending with Witte and Stolypin, who sought to adapt imperial Russian society in one degree or another to the requirements of the modern

From Cyril E. Black, "The Nature of Imperial Russian Society," *Slavic Review,* XX (December 1961), 574–82. By permission of Cyril Black and the *Slavic Review.*

world. Their views were set forth in speeches, reports, memoranda, and statutes, and perhaps in deeds more than in words. The second source of intellectual activity was that represented by the intelligentsia, who almost by definition were disassociated and not infrequently alienated from the governing circles. The intelligentsia left a fascinating heritage of speculation and interpretation which reflected a broad understanding of European society and a deep concern for the destiny of the Russian people. They had a profound influence on the development of Russian society during the period of the empire, since their works were read and discussed by all educated people. They nevertheless remained until the end alienated from official Russia, which bore the burden of responsibility and deserves much of the credit for the extent to which Russian society was transformed by the time of the First World War. The intelligentsia as a group did not gain access to political power until the fall of the empire, and this access was terminated for all but a few when the Bolsheviks began to suppress deviations from orthodoxy in the early 1920's. In the realm of scholarship Russia joined the world of modern knowledge in the course of the eighteenth and nineteenth centuries and made distinguished original contributions.

The history of Russian thought in the nineteenth century as a general phenomenon has yet to be written. Much able work has been done on individual writers and on the leading intellectual movements, such as the Decembrists, the Slavophiles, the Populists, and the Marxists. The thought of the reforming officials has not, however, received comparable attention. Neither the prerevolutionary intelligentsia nor the writers of the Soviet Union have been attracted to this subject, for reasons which are not hard to find, and Western scholars are only now beginning to explore it. Interest in intellectual history seems to have been concerned principally with a desire to study the background of the political revolution of 1917, and this has resulted in a serious neglect of the fundamental process of political, economic, and social change as a central issue in Russian thought.

In the political sphere the adoption of modern institutions in Russia can be seen in the many reforms which had the purpose of rationalizing the system of law and administration, integrating the various territories and social strata, and establishing a closer rapport between state and society to the end that political decisions could be effectively formulated, communicated, and implemented. The reforms of the eighteenth century had performed a similar function for the state itself, and it was now a question of extending this process to the entire society. The codification of the laws by Speransky was the first significant step in this second phase, and it was followed in the 1860's by an extensive reform of the judiciary and local government and of the administrative system of the central government. As late as 1905, however, the state had relatively few direct administrative contacts with the peasants except for a rather scanty police force and the land captains established in 1889. Peasant affairs were handled largely by the peasants themselves. The administration of the Stolypin land settlement required the government for the first time in its history to establish organs for administering directly at the local level policies ultimately affecting a large proportion of the population and involving the co-ordination of several ministries. This was a very late development, however, and the weakness of the imperial bureaucracy was soon revealed in the harsh test of war.

The effort to transform the political system of imperial Russia along the lines pioneered by the societies of Western Europe provoked a struggle among several trends of thought. One was that of the supporters of the traditional system as it had been consolidated in the eighteenth and early nineteenth centuries. This was the view of the imperial family and its immediate entourage, and it had strong support in the army and bureaucracy and in the cabinet, even when that body was headed by a reforming minister. The reforms of the 1860's had indeed been launched by the emperor himself, but more in the Petrine spirit of trying to achieve a new conservative stability than with a view to a thoroughgoing social reconstruction. This approach continued to have strong official support until the end, and one may well attribute the catastrophic character of the fall of the empire to the stubbornness with which one group of its leaders resisted change.

Another main trend was the very large one represented by those both in the government and among the intelligentsia who favored fundamental change by evolutionary means and looked to models ranging from England and France to Prussia and Japan. The diversities of their various programs make it difficult to contain these many groups in a single category, but the Fundamental Laws of 1906 provided them with a more or less acceptable basis for action and there was a significant degree of continuity from the four successive Dumas to the Provisional Government. Included also in this category were the leaders of the national minorities who demanded a degree of self-government. Only the Poles insisted unconditionally on independence. This issue has been beclouded by war, revolution, and civil war, but it appears that under "normal" circumstances the leaders of the other minority peoples would in all likelihood have been satisfied on the eve of the First World War with some form of federalism.

A third trend was composed of those who had no faith in evolutionary changes within the framework of the empire. This was the view of the Bolsheviks and many Socialist Revolutionaries, who saw their political role principally as a destructive one so long as the empire survived. The final arbiter among these various approaches, as it turned out, was the First World War. The strains of the conflict eroded the political structure of the empire, and in so doing undermined the prospects for evolutionary change within its framework. The collapse of the empire opened the way for a revolutionary approach, and the revolutionaries were much more at home than the liberals in the ensuing chaos.

Among the changes which occurred during the last half-century of the empire, those in the intellectual and political realm have attracted the most attention, but the remarkable economic growth in its later decades deserves equal emphasis. Agricultural production, which had not been able to keep up with the growth of the population during the first half of the century, increased much more rapidly, especially after the 1880's. Not only did agricultural production surpass the rate at which the population was growing, but it was also significantly diversified to include industrial crops and potatoes. The expansion of industrial production was of course much more rapid, with an annual average rate of growth of somewhat over 5 per cent for the period 1885–1913. The rate for the 1890's, the period of most rapid growth, was surpassed only by that of Japan, the United States, and Sweden. Underlying the increased rates of growth in agriculture and industry was the construction of an extensive railroad network, which grew from 1,000 miles in 1860 to 40,000 miles at the time of the First World War. In terms of national income, the Russian rate of growth for the period as a whole was higher than that of the United Kingdom, France, and Italy, somewhat below that of Germany, and considerably below that of the United States and Japan. On a per capita basis Russia's position was of course less favorable, owing to the rapid growth of her population. By the time of the First World War real income per capita was about the same as that of Italy, which means that it was still a great deal lower than that of the advanced industrial societies.

Although Russia had thus in no sense attained a leading position as an industrial society at the time of the First World War, what is significant is that by the 1880's it was launched on a pattern of economic growth comparable in rate and dimensions to that of the more advanced societies. It should also be noted that this was very largely the achievement of the imperial government, which took the initiative and bore the main burden of building railroads and supplying capital to industry, and also provided the principal market for the output of heavy industry. No doubt the sovereign and the conservative-minded courtiers and ministers, like Peter the Great in his day, still thought of industrialization principally as a means of bolstering the autocratic system. The leading cabinet members and high officials, however, had a vision of a Russia transformed into a modern industrial society. Their goal may be said to have been of a West European character, but their methods were quite different. Little attention was devoted to agriculture, and such income as it normally provided was channeled into industry. Railroads and heavy industry were favored as against consumer goods. Modern technology was imported from the West to make up for deficiencies in skilled labor, and economies were made in management and supervision by concentrating production in large plants. A not inconsiderable role in this growth was played by private entrepreneurs and small businessmen, but the pace was set by the government and by the large enterprises which it controlled or patronized. Indeed, it was the role of the government as planner, investor, entrepreneur, and consumer which distinguished economic growth in Russia from that in the societies which started earlier.

This economic growth was accomplished by fundamental social changes. The urban population grew from 7 to 20 million during the last fifty years of the empire, the rigid system of social stratification disintegrated rapidly, and the foundations were laid for a new stratum of professional people, businessmen, and officials. This "middle class" was drawn from all of the traditional strata. The nobles, clergy, and townsmen were naturally the principal sources of recruitment for this new stratum at the start, but the peasantry and workers were gradually drawn into it and represented in the long run its principal reserve of manpower. The nobles lost much of their distinctive position in the last decades of the empire and, with the exception of the relatively few families of great wealth, did not gain much advantage from their remaining formal privileges in the evolving industrial society. At the same time the industrial working class grew apace, and numbered some 3.5 million at the end of this period. In 1913, according to the official classification, 70.2 per cent of the population were farmers, 16.7 per cent were wage and salary workers, 7.2 per cent were craftsmen, 3.6 per cent were self-employed townsmen, and 2.3 per cent were military and others.

The institutions of higher education were the chief training ground for this new class, and their enrollment in proportion to the population increased more than nine times between 1885 and 1914. The increase in secondary-school enrollment was even greater, and by the time of the First World War Russia had made substantial progress toward a system of universal elementary education. The social mobility accompanying the growth in higher education is reflected in the fact that the proportion of children of peasants, craftsmen, and workers enrolled in the universities grew from 15.7 per cent in 1880 to 38.8 per cent in 1914, and in the higher technical institutes was 54 per cent in the latter year. The officer corps was no doubt the most conservative branch of the bureaucracy, but it appears that by the end of the empire a majority of the new officers came from nonnoble families as did some of the leading generals in the First World War. In recording these changes it should be noted that this rapid growth in educational opportunities and social mobility was not achieved without a momentous struggle. In the central government the reformers waged a constant battle with the traditionalists, and were strongly aided by the increasingly effective support which they received from the local government institutions, the municipalities, and the Duma. At the time of the First World War, Russia was still a country where 78 per cent of the population was agricultural and rural illiteracy was high. The changes of the last half century had been so rapid, however, that contemporary reforming statesmen could look forward with confidence to the day when the empire would attain the level of achievement of Western societies.

Something should also be said about the personality changes which may have accompanied this general process. National character in the sense that it is used by the social psychologists is a controversial concept which is still in an early stage of formulation, and one hesitates to venture into a territory so ridden with pitfalls. Yet it is clear that the personality of the individual reflects the character of his upbringing in the family setting, which in turn depends on the larger social context. When the latter undergoes the drastic changes represented by urbanization, one would expect the family and its individual members to be vitally affected. In the case of the Great Russian people, for example, it has been maintained that the characteristically patriarchal peasant family tended to produce a personality which was markedly ambivalent. This is to say that the Great Russian personality contained simultaneously elements of great vitality and serious depression, which may be explained as resulting from a family setting in which an awesome father was both feared and resisted. As a peasant society with these characteristics is urbanized, with the mother as an urban worker gaining a position of authority more nearly equal to that of the father, an altered family setting is produced in which the children are exposed to somewhat different influences and will develop correspondingly different personalities. This example suggests what is meant by the effects of social change on personality, and it also reveals the difficulties which confront one in trying to deal with Russia in these terms. Russia was a vastly complex empire with many traditional cultures, of which the Great Russian was only one. Moreover, the available studies deal principally with the Soviet period, and there is little factual data from earlier decades to draw on. One may argue that Chekhov, Gorky, and their literary colleagues did a pretty good job of reporting social change at the family level without benefit of professional training in the behavioral sciences, but it is difficult for a historian to generalize on the basis of their findings. It is also clear that the impact of social change on personality was at its very earliest stages in the last decades of the empire, and that one would not expect to find general manifestations of a transformation of national character in Russia until well into the twentieth century. Under the circumstances the best one can do is to call attention to this important aspect of social history and to regret that one cannot do it justice.

II

The interaction of traditional and modern institutions and values in imperial Russian society should be considered in terms both of its general implications and of its particular significance for the crisis provoked by the collapse of the empire in the First World War.

The prevailing Western approach between the two world wars to Russian developments was to assume that the institutions characteristic of the more advanced societies of the West represented the model which other societies were destined to follow. There was therefore a tendency to judge the empire as well as its successors by the extent to which they adopted the Western pattern in such matters as civil liberties, representative government, education, and the role of the state in economic growth. By this standard the empire was reactionary, the Provisional Government had liberal aspirations, and the Soviet Union represented a bewildering combination of modern and traditional elements. In the course of the past quarter of a century many other societies have entered and some have completed the experimental phase of adapting the traditional to the modern, and the process of transformation can now be seen as a much more complex matter than one of simply duplicating Western institutions. It seems clear that there are certain functions which all modern societies must perform — political decision-making effective for the entire population, sufficient savings to permit a reasonable rate of economic growth, education, social mobility, and so on — and perhaps most important of all, a value system compatible with the necessary institutional changes. It is also clear, however, that there is a wide degree of variety in the extent to which the diverse traditional institutional systems are adaptable to the functions of modern societies. No society can avoid very profound changes as it modernizes, but some traditional institutions are much more adaptable than others.

What is significant in the case of Russia is that its traditional institutional system was different from those of the societies of Western Europe, as indeed it was from those of non-European societies as well. In Western Europe modern political institutions, for example, evolved from those of feudalism into a characteristic form of liberal government in which political power was shared by elected representatives and a permanent civil service. In Russia, by contrast, the starting point was not a feudal system but an autocratic state which had characteristically exercised very extensive political functions. It was not difficult for this state, in the generation after the defeat in the Crimea, to initiate a very fundamental reorientation of national life. Between 1861 and 1917 the autocracy in Russia put into effect a series of reforms which resemble in many respects those achieved by very different methods in France between 1789 and 1848 — if one may risk an historical analogy. To extend the analogy a step further, one may suggest that the autocratic state in Russia played a role similar not only to that of the middle class and the Napoleonic empire in France but also to that of the samurai in Japan, the Young Turks in the Ottoman Empire, the army officers in Egypt, and the European-educated politicians in Africa today. Modernizing political leadership may take many forms, and the alternatives available to political leaders cannot fail to be profoundly affected by the traditional political institutions which a society has inherited from earlier centuries. This is not to assert an institutional or a cultural determinism. It is rather to suggest that, however similar the ultimate functional goals, political leaders in different societies are likely to proceed by different routes.

It would be outside the limits set for this paper to venture beyond the fall of the empire in February/March, 1917, but it is relevant to discuss the bearing on subsequent developments of the changes which the empire was undergoing in its final decades. It is well enough to attribute the fall of the empire to the strains of the First World War, for the connection between the two is clear, but it is also necessary to note that the crisis was not so great that a more effective government might not have been able to cope with it. The vital struggle in the last decades of the empire was that which was going on within the government between those who supported the traditional autocracy to the bitter end, and those who favored the transformation of Russia into a modern bureaucratic and constitutional state. The Wittes and Stolypins were still separated by a wide gap from the liberals, but the gap was perhaps no wider than that which separated them from the emperor. The lines dividing the various conservative and liberal conceptions of an evolutionary constitutionalism were becoming increasingly blurred in the last years of the empire, and much would have depended on the leadership which might have emerged.

The war came at a time when these conflicts between the emperor and his critics within the government were still unresolved, and in fact it only served to make them more bitter. The fragmentation of Russian politics at this stage was such that the collapse of the autocracy in 1917 resulted in a situation in which no alternative had any wide support. There was of course a significant group of leaders favoring parliamentary democracy who had gained political experience in the Duma and in local government, but the political methods which they favored were not generally understood or accepted. Where parliamentary democracy has been successful it has in fact been a value system widely supported by many elements of a society rather than one reflecting the interests of a particular social stratum. The vast majority of Russians — whether peasants, workers, bureaucrats, officers, or professional people — were not generally familiar with the values and techniques of parliamentary democracy. To this extent the task of leaders favoring parliamentary methods in 1917 was infinitely more difficult than that of those prepared to rely on force. This does not necessarily mean that the empire might not under other circumstances have developed into a political democracy of the type familiar in the West, or even that something resembling such a system may not yet develop in Russia at some future time. It means only that, at the time the empire collapsed, the balance of domestic political experience weighed heavily in favor of those leaders who were prepared to employ authoritarian methods.

Nicholas II Was a Bulwark Against Reform

DONALD W. TREADGOLD

Donald W. Treadgold, educated at Harvard and Oxford, is Professor of Modern Russian History at the University of Washington in Seattle and for some years was Managing Editor of the scholarly journal, the *Slavic Review*. In addition to *Lenin and His Rivals*, Professor Treadgold is author of *The Great Siberian Migration* and *Twentieth Century Russia*. His painstakingly objective analysis of Nicholas II's character and political ideas well illustrates what is generally considered to have been the fatal flaw of Russian autocracy—the stubborn incompetence of its last Tsar. If for no other reason, revolution, it would appear, was necessary to rid Russia of this ruler who clung so stolidly to the past and stood in the way of intelligent reform.

I

THE last of the eighteen Romanov autocrats who had ruled Russia since the Time of Troubles (1613) was practically unique in the Western world of the 20th century. He tried his level best to be a good eighteenth century Emperor. No one can say he might not have succeeded two hundred years earlier, if only he had had the intelligence and strength of will which some of his ancestors and not a few of their foreign wives had possessed. In his own era he never fully realized the problems which faced him. His one successful political act, promulgation of the October Manifesto, was an accident whose import and effect — it was no less than to save his throne temporarily — he scarcely guessed. His family and court lived in an atmosphere of simplicity, devotion, and utter lack of comprehension of the world outside which has lent itself without difficulty to depiction by many writers as sheer fantasy. Personally he was as conscientious as he was unapproachable — probably his English collie Iman gave him as much companionship as any human being. He was too densely self-assured to be very maladroit. With his family and friends, with a common Siberian hunter or with a "man of God," he might display charm. With his own highest officials, he might be gruff and preoccupied, and only too often any kind words or unusual attentiveness to an official might be the prelude to his abrupt and curt dismissal. Industrialism was beyond his understanding, revolutionaries were to him simply manifestations of evil to be crushed at any cost, good government not an ideal to be sought but an irrelevance compared to the fulfilment of the commands of his ancestors and the maintenance of the loyalty of the Russian people to his own person.

Politically, he was completely at sea. In his public utterances he never thought it necessary to define his policy, or to allow that there might be such a thing as his "policy." During the Revolution of 1905, an opposition publisher collected his entire public addresses from 1894 to 1906 and printed them in one thin pamphlet, with the sarcastic foreword, "not many words, but much food for thought is provided. In the speeches of the Monarch there is no place for wordiness, long rhetorical phrases; there is no place for flowery pretentious sentences: the real distinction of these speeches is their lack of artifice, completely epic simplicity, straightforwardness of argument." A typical "speech" may be quoted in full, his welcome to an army delegation on 16 August 1898:

I am very glad to see you again. I thank you for your service, especially the Cavaliers of St. George. I drink to your health, brothers, and happiness. Hurrah!

Nicholas II was of course not the idiot that this pamphlet made him appear to be. The notion that a twentieth-century monarch must devote some attention to politics was simply foreign to him. This might not have been fatal had he been willing to select, or let someone else select, ministers who could provide efficiency, direction or continuity of policy in the conduct of affairs. When he did happen across a Witte, he refused to trust him. When he found a Stolypin, he became gradually estranged from him. Rasputin inspired his trust not so much in governmental as in his private affairs; and if a man could heal his bleeding son and save the life of the sovereign heir, could his inspiration not be followed in the tedious realm of politics?

Politics may have been dull and tedious to Nicholas II, but there ought to have been nothing which claimed more of his attention if only to secure the survival of himself and his dynasty. Whatever economic transformation was sweeping over the ancient social structure of Russia — and we have already paid some attention to this matter — the place in which the fate of Russia was to be decided was the political arena. To this the Marxists, although they believed politics to be a function of economics, would nevertheless agree. They would of course deny, however, the contention here made that the intelligentsia, which was making a bid to become a new ruling class, was a group whose common distinguishing feature was political interests and activity rather than economic origin or status.

In the minds of all the intelligentsia, the questions which were to determine the future of Russia were political questions. What needed to be done to better the conditions of the "people"? What sort of regime was necessary to do it? What legal rights and privileges ought a citizen to enjoy if any social benefits were to be securely enjoyed? Upon what source of authority should legislative action to these ends depend?

The Tsardom never got beyond the first question, and scarcely seemed even to take that one seriously until the Revolution of 1905 was almost upon it. The actions of the government were always in the rear of the march of events. When, for a moment, the Tsar stumbled abreast of the fast-moving situation with the October Manifesto, he failed to repeat his chance success. Convinced he had already gone farther than he needed, he sulked through the period of parliamentarism which followed. Only on the very eve of his downfall had he one last flash of insight, when he confided to an anachronism of a different sort, Rodzianko, that everything he had done for twenty years had been wrong. For two decades Tsarism was consistently too late, and this was no accident. It was not that its machinery was necessarily inadequate. Its bureaucracy was no better or worse than many others. Its political assumptions were simply unrealistic.

Nicholas II assumed a normal condition for Russia in which a tranquil people were loyal to an absolute monarch, and any temporary abnormality was taken to be the work of "troublemakers." Hence the Tsardom showed an efficiency in following the traces of the revolutionaries and in penetrating their most secret plans which was quite absent in its efforts to alleviate the economic difficulties of any social class, including the gentry, its erstwhile bulwark. Once a concession had been made toward popular representation in the shape of the Duma, the autocracy still refused to normalize its relations with the parliament — not even the conservative Third Duma, under the prime ministership of Russia's ablest statesman in generations, Peter Stolypin. Before 1906, the government tried to rule the country by ignoring any direct expression of public opinion and refusing to admit any direct participation of even the more conservative "public men" from the ranks of "society." Political issues, if they could not be ignored entirely, were deemed beyond the competence of those outside government. Even during the parliamentary period following 1906, the Tsar never conceded that there was any question about the ultimate location of authority. Before and after 1906, it lay in his own Person. Any alternative he could imagine only as attaching to some universal catastrophe which he did not expect. He did not believe in the possibility of revolution enough to fear it deeply.

II

Nicholas II hated revolutionaries, but despised liberals. He did not understand the argument that reforms might avoid revolution, for this was a political argument. He did not listen to the pleas of liberals to alter his governmental system because they had no right to speak on such matters. Their toying with Western notions of "constitutions" and so forth he regarded as un-Russian, idle nonsense, and pernicious, no matter what protestations of loyalty were used to cloak such demands. The liberals had asked his grandfather in 1878 to grant "those same blessings" to the Russians as he had already granted the Bulgarians — that is, a constitution. When he himself came to the throne in January 1895 an attempt to repeat such a plea to new, young imperial ears was sharply repulsed by an allusion to "senseless dreams of the participation of zemstvo men in legislative affairs." When at the end of the 90's the liberals decided to ignore the Tsar and refuse to talk to him further about public improvement, they were only recognizing an accomplished fact. It was not that they were dissatisfied with his replies; he had made none. He had simply refused to carry on a discussion. He drove the Right Liberals into the camp of the revolutionaries; many of the Left Liberals were there already.

As Emperor, his policy was accordingly nonexistent. He took what his father bequeathed to him, including the institutions of Autocracy, and assumed their suitability and permanence. What governmental policy there was emanated from his ministers, and often there was not much. Soon after his accession he appointed, to replace a Minister of Interior who displeased his strong-willed mother, the Dowager Empress, an inconspicuously endowed bureaucrat named Ivan Logginovich Goremykin. The Interior Minister was then the official who, more than anyone else, was in charge of domestic policy. The other two candidates Nicholas considered for this important post in 1895 were Sipiagin and Plehve, who were stigmatized by even his ultra-reactionary old counsellor, Pobedonostsev, as "fool" and "scoundrel" respectively. That did not prevent the Emperor from appointing precisely these two men successively to the post following Goremykin. Both were assassinated in office. By the time Nicholas had to choose another man, in the summer of 1904, the Russo-Japanese War had begun and the revolution was about to break out. In fact the Emperor was never close to any of these men, and he had no scruples about finding grounds for dismissing any of his ministers. It is not certain he understood the function of a minister, but it is probable that as far as he did, he disapproved the notion.

III

Always uncertain as to how far the Emperor stood behind them, never able to interpret his approval of one particular measure as general support for their policies, the Imperial ministers undertook to contend with a growing strike movement which within a decade turned into a movement of mass political opposition. Goremykin was at once confronted with the problem of dealing with the growing pains of industrialism, Russia's first large-scale strikes, which swept the factories of St. Petersburg. The aims of these strikes were chiefly better working conditions. Some Marxists who took part wished the strikes had broader aims and said they ought to have, but the political element in them was so far negligible. The government therefore was not making any concessions as to its own power when it passed a maximum-hours law under pressure of the strikers. After this minor victory the workers hesitated, debating the question of what strikes could do for them. The question was shelved, however, by the depression which overtook Russia's booming industry in 1899.

Now and only now did the workers begin to listen seriously to their would-be leaders among the revolutionaries, but mass strikes were for the moment out of the question. The initiative which the factory workers were forced to drop was taken up vigorously, however, by university students. Their organized protests were sometimes nominally directed against restrictions on academic freedom, but their political character was apparent to all. The students were the vanguard of the intelligentsia, and it was they who began the "Liberation Movement."

Goremykin, who had an early reputation for liberalism of a sort, was by the time of his interior ministry at least as lazy as liberal. He did declare his support of the territorial extension of the zemstvo. Witte opposed the measure, and declared the zemstvo to be fundamentally incompatible with Autocracy. He later hinted that this was "Aesopean language" meaning "down with Autocracy" rather than "down with the zemstvo," but the effect of the argument in 1899 was quite the reverse. Goremykin's stand in favor of the zemstvo was enough to bring about his replacement by Sipiagin. This pliant tool of the gentry, no less "foolish" than he had been in 1895, once distinguished himself by falling on his knees drunk in a Petersburg club and praying aloud: "O God, it is not I who am guilty as to our household expenses . . ."

The student demonstrations of 1899 were suppressed only to recommence in a year. When the government issued restrictive "temporary rules" for the universities, one student, acting alone, retaliated by killing the minister of education in February 1901. The recrudescence of terrorism was met by a concession. General Vannovskii replaced the dead Bogolepov with instructions to exert "heartfelt care" over the Tsar's obstreperous student subjects. The movement, nevertheless, was already out of hand. The students were now joined by workers in their fiery meetings in favor of "freedom" and "justice." A great strike in the Obukhov factory of Petersburg really alarmed the government, which was this time itself the owner-employer. In the autumn and spring, worker demonstrations were almost continual. The problem of how Sipiagin was to meet all this was solved by his assassination on 2 April 1902, this time not an act of an isolated individual but the result of a systematic plan of the Socialist Revolutionary Battle Organization.

The "scoundrel," Viacheslav von Plehve, a completely unprincipled but clever man, now replaced Sipiagin the "fool." He had already made himself unpopular as secretary of State for Finland during the period of attack on Finnish liberties, and as head of the police. While holding the latter post in 1901 he conceived the unique experiment of allowing one of his agents, Zubatov, to organize a union of mechanics in Moscow to work for improved working conditions. Zubatov tried to head off political discussion and tried to convince his membership that revolution was unnecessary by urging them to read Eduard Bernstein. This venture in "police socialism" soon became entirely too popular to manage. When the Zubatov agent in Odessa was discovered to be an actual leader of the great strikes of 1903 the whole scheme was hurriedly abandoned.

Plehve entered the interior ministry to find that an ancient bugaboo of Tsarism had after long disuse reappeared — peasant revolt, which began to send wisps of smoke curling up from Kharkov and Poltava provinces. The revolutionaries hoped — and the government feared — that although these spontaneous outbreaks had no political aims, it might be possible to graft politics onto them. Politics, the government reasoning ran, was originated by "troublemakers," and the agency to deal with such gentlemen was the police. Police methods, after all, were the forte of Plehve. He not only repressed the peasant riots with severity, but punished the governor of Poltava for being insufficiently harsh. Of course the governor of Kharkov, who was severe indeed with the insurgents, was promptly assassinated, but this merely provided an opportunity to punish someone else — the assassins. The Tsar himself appeared before a council of village elders at Kursk, sternly admonishing them to remember their duty to God and the state, which meant ignoring the seductions of "troublemakers." . . .

Plehve's methods failed utterly to halt unrest. He refused to admit that arresting disorder was anything but a sort of vermin-killing operation which the agencies of state could handle. He saw no need for enlisting public support, for that ought to be forthcoming by right. Therefore he even snubbed the extremely moderate zemstvo group which, under the leadership of the conscientiously loyal Dmitrii Shipov, attempted to indicate what reforms were needed without venturing to ask any law-making powers for themselves. When the zemstvo men held a cautiously conducted congress in May 1902, Plehve not only rebuffed its proposals but in retaliation forced Shipov out of his post as president of the Moscow zemstvo. Plehve's only potential collaborators were thus silenced for the duration of his ministry. On the other hand, professional men and more radical zemstvoists spoke out the more sharply against him. In January 1904 a congress of physicians startled the public by denouncing the government as responsible for a multitude of evils up to disease itself. A few days later, the Japanese sank much of the Russian fleet in Port Arthur and the Russo-Japanese war had begun.

From Plehve's viewpoint this was no calamity. Since all else was of no avail, he had decided on a "small victorious war" in which mighty Russia would swiftly and gloriously whip her Oriental neighbor. This would divert attention from the siren calls of the troublemakers and rally the nation round its duty to the Tsar which it seemed inexplicably to be forgetting. However, instead of transmuting revolutionary energies into patriotic ones, the war had exactly the opposite effect. Leaders of all branches of the "Liberation Movement" preached open defeatism. Possibly a military victory or two would have rallied some of the opposition to support the government, but at any rate the war turned out to be the kind opposite to that anticipated, with a string of crushing defeats instead of one smashing triumph. After each successive defeat the opposition spoke out more sharply. Port Arthur fell after a long siege, and then came "Bloody Sunday." The Russian army was sent reeling at Mukden, followed by spring zemstvo congresses. The Baltic fleet was sunk on arrival in Tsushima Strait, and the July zemstvo congress at once began to talk like a revolutionary assembly. The Peace of Portsmouth in August was too late to reverse the trend of events.

Plehve did not live to see the end of his military venture. He was murdered on July 15 by a revolutionary plot in which one of his own agents, Azef, was involved. Police methods had not only killed their own author. They had failed to check the multiplication of the radical vermin, who proved impervious to Plehve's cleverest poisons. Worst of all, their use had consumed priceless months in which the opportunity to embark on serious reforms had been sacrificed.

Nicholas II now, as in the case of the Vannovskii appointment in 1901, appeared to give ground to terrorism. He replaced Plehve by the mild-mannered Mirskii, who at once spoke of having "confidence in society" — i.e., *obshchestvo*. To buttress itself the regime would deign to trust some of the enlightened aristocrats. The need of inspiring the trust of the public *in* the regime was still ignored. Relieved of their bitterest enemy, Plehve, the zemstvo men convened a congress at which they adopted what Miliukov called (looking for an English parallel) "the famous Petition of Right," demanding sweeping reforms including an all-Russian legislative assembly. The nation's intelligentsia responded to this call with even sharper demands in a "banquet campaign" on the model of the French in 1848. Not merely a parliament, but a "Four-Tail Constituent Assembly" became the universal slogan, shared by all sections of the opposition from moderate liberals to revolutionaries. The drawing together of these disparate groups, crossing the line of social respectability between the "underground" and "society," was symbolized by an inter-party opposition congress in Paris which recognized the common task of struggling for a "democratic regime."

Thus not suddenly as mere protest at the Port Arthur defeat, but amid an engulfing wave of public agitation, came the tragic procession of St. Petersburg workers of 9 January 1905. Organized by the police agent Father Gapon, these unfortunates marched peacefully and loyally to the Winter Palace to present a gigantic petition to their Sovereign, only to shed their loyalty along with their blood as the police massacred them. This catastrophe, dubbed "Bloody Sunday," was widely recognized as the "beginning of the revolution." A new wave of strikes, initiated by Baku oil workers in December, spurted abruptly. Students left universities. Peasant riots began again in Oriol.

Once more the Tsar seemed to yield at the appearance of violence. The commission of Senator Shidlovskii was set up to investigate the workers' grievances, and on 18 February the Tsar issued three acts of strangely contradictory substance. This habit of hedging on the market of revolution was one established even earlier. In December the Tsar had issued an ukase ordering his ministers to consider reforms giving the peasant equal rights with the other classes, the worker more secure labor conditions, the zemstvos added independence, and so forth. Yet only two days later there followed an Imperial reprimand threatening the zemstvos for considering questions outside their competence — echoing the "senseless dreams" rebuke of a decade before. Now, two months after that, Nicholas issued, first, a manifesto sternly summoning the people to rally around the Autocracy of their fathers; second, a rescript to A. G. Bulygin (the nominal interior minister, actually fronting for D. F. Trepov who had the Tsar's trust) directing him to work out a plan for a consultative assembly of "men worthiest of the people's trust";

third, an ukase to the Senate, ordering the consideration of any new projects for reform submitted by loyal citizens. The Russian citizen contemplating these three contradictory acts might well have felt puzzlement as to the Tsar's intentions. Many just seized on the third as official sanction for the broadest kind of public discussion and agitation. Maklakov declares, "from the time of this ukase . . . the autocracy's fate was sealed." The offer of a consultative assembly was ignored. The zemstvo leaders, already in the forefront of the "respectable" opposition, pushed ahead with congress after congress throughout 1905 in which they steadily increased their pressure on the Tsardom for reform. Members of the professions (and some skilled trades) organized "unions" which in turn joined to form a Union of Unions. A section of the peasantry banded together in an All-Russian Peasant Union. Even big industrialists met publicly to demand constitutional reform. Most vocal and definite of all were of course the opposition parties, whose activities form another part of our story.

More disturbing even than these unruly but peaceful assemblies were the spreading strikes, riots, and even mutinies in the armed forces — notably the temporarily successful uprising on the cruiser Potiomkin in June, the rebellion of the Kronstadt sailors in October, and the Sevastopol mutiny in November.

Again the Tsar retreated a pace. Faced by the disloyalty of almost the entire vocal population, he was unable to delay any longer publishing an act establishing a State Duma of the kind foreshadowed in the Bulygin rescript. It was to be an assembly of estates, with landowners, townsmen, and peasants voting in curias, while 27 cities were on a separate franchise. Deputies were to be chosen in from two to four stages, depending on the curia. Urban workers and lower middle classes had no vote, and the Duma itself was restricted both in its own powers and by being designated as the lower of two legislative houses, as the existing Imperial Council was transformed into an upper chamber.

Jeers and curses greeted this act of 6 August. Public clamor mounted despite the signing of the Peace of Portsmouth, ending the war with Japan, for which the Russian negotiator, Witte, was made a count. The peace, as with every other act of the Tsar in the revolution, came too late to have any effect on public opinion. It did, however, free troops for the eventual repression of the revolution.

The fate of the country now in effect passed out of the hands of the authorities, and descended into the hands of the striking workers. Numbering 200,000 in May, they had diminished in September only to grow sharply again. On 7 October the workers on the Moscow-Kazan railroad struck, and in about a week transport and communication throughout the country were paralyzed. On 12 October a Council (*Soviet*) of Workers Deputies was organized in St. Petersburg, dominated by Mensheviks but officially nonpartisan, a political body which announced a general strike with the purpose of compelling the Tsar to summon a Four-Tail Constituent Assembly. Russia's workers responded by bringing economic life to a dead halt.

After four days of this impasse, the Tsar appeared to have surrendered. His famous October Manifesto, ambiguous as it was, had a tone very different from his previous half-measures. Count Witte, back from Portsmouth, had persuaded him to promise freedom of speech, press, and assembly, and to convert the Duma into a legislative body whose consent was necessary to enact any law. Witte himself became Russia's first Prime Minister.

Was the October Manifesto, likewise, too late? Much of the burden of our story lies here. . . . Briefly the Manifesto was the moment when the Tsar overtook the onrushing revolution, when he for once, in spite of himself and only on the urging of the ever afterwards unforgiven Witte, stepped out of the role of the divine Autocrat and into the unaccustomed realm of politics. . . .

Was there to be a Duma? There was. It was a question not of political wisdom but personal honor to the Tsar who evidently had no thought of retracting his promise — in the sense he interpreted it. In February it was announced that the assembly would convene on 27 April and the electoral campaign began at once. Only four days before the opening of the Duma, the Tsar issued the Fundamental Laws which were supposed to implement the promises of the October Manifesto. But the "freedoms" were found to be hedged about by limitations, and the Duma was discovered to have an unwelcome partner in legislation — the Imperial Council (the upper chamber as in the Bulygin project). This body was to be henceforth half nominated by the Sovereign, half elected by certain privileged bodies. As if this was not enough to hamstring the Duma, the Tsar retained a veto power over legislation not to mention complete control of the armed forces and foreign policy. Secure in his still autocratic authority, as he thought, Nicholas II now found courage to dismiss the importunate Witte. He appointed a new cabinet headed by the indolent Goremykin, but distinguished by a new, strong personality: Peter Stolypin, ex-governor of Saratov, as interior minister.

The "Duma of people's hopes" convened on schedule. Boycotted by most of the revolutionaries, it was dominated by the liberals, and the Right was scarcely perceptible. This kind of body was of course anathema to the Emperor, who nevertheless managed to bring himself to receive the deputies on 27 April in the Winter Palace and deliver them a short, moderately phrased address. The Speech from the Throne, as men with a fondness for English methods dubbed it, might have been given to a Bulygin-type Duma had one ever convened. He spoke of the deputies as those "very best men whom I gave my beloved subjects the order to elect," whom he had called upon for "cooperation" in the work of legislation. A "new regime" was hard to divine behind such phrases, among which there was to be found no mention of "constitution" or "parliament" and in which "freedom" was carefully coupled with "order." The angry address which the Duma composed in reply to this Speech was entrusted for delivery to a deputation which the Tsar flatly refused even to receive. Goremykin was sent to chastise the assembly on 13 May. The liberals retorted by declaring no confidence in the ministry, and for the rest of the session government and Duma were openly hostile to each other.

Nevertheless the majority of deputies, believing they could rely on the country's support, resolutely advanced to "legislate" — to push through reform laws which the Tsar would not dare to veto. The chief issue, that of land reform, was the object of several radical proposals by Leftist deputies; the government's own drafts on the subject were simply ignored. The legislative impasse, in view of the riotous impatience of the peasants, was anxiously considered from both sides. From the side of the government, D. F. Trepov and Stolypin tried to persuade the liberals to enter a ministry which had so far remained entirely composed of bureaucrats, despite the institution of a "constitutional" system. The liberals refused to share the power and the talks failed.

From the side of the Duma, the majority, faced with government warnings against a radical land bill, adopted in the beginning of July an open appeal to the people for support of their agrarian project. Such a "disloyal" act was taken by the Tsar as pretext for abruptly dissolving the First Duma — therein acting quite constitutionally. On the same day, 8 July, the Goremykin cabinet retired and Stolypin became Prime Minister. The government was obviously determined on firmness.

Forthwith many Duma deputies fled to Finland and issued the "Vyborg Manifesto" to the people of the Russian Empire, exhorting them to support the Duma by refusing to pay taxes or furnish recruits. The lack of response was a great disappointment to the "legislators" who had regarded themselves as popular tribunes. Isolated mutinies in Sveaborg and Kronstadt and scattered strikes took place, but the Revolution of 1905 was for all practical purposes at an end. Realists saw clearly that the summer of 1906 had put an end for the time being to hopes for ending Autocracy by mass action. The next year, 1907, there was returned a "Duma of people's wrath" with large revolutionary representation, but a sizeable Rightist group as well, and the percentage of deputies who opposed the government remained the same as in the First Duma. Stolypin sat firmly in the saddle of power, and he used it not only to dismiss the Second Duma, but to alter the suffrage law in such a manner that he would not have to dismiss the Third.

For one fateful moment Autocracy had tottered on the edge of oblivion. At that moment the Emperor was pushed, not into the abyss by the revolutionaries, but into the use of a political weapon by his new prime minister. The publication of the October Manifesto, inadequate in itself but so clearly out of character with Nicholas's previous conduct that it inspired false hopes in the widest circles, gave the regime the breathing space it needed to regroup its forces for the only kind of campaign which the Tsar found congenial: police methods. So Nicholas was saved from destruction, but never understood why. His reformists, Witte and Stolypin, were not liberals, but that did not preserve them from his profound suspicion to the degree that they insisted that police methods were insufficient to calm the revolutionary storm. The October Manifesto might have been too late even if it had marked a shift to a course of political action — we cannot be sure. What we can be sure of is that the Emperor Nicholas II never realized that only politics could save him from the attack of the politically-minded intellectuals, and this realization came only after the deluge had overtaken him in the Great Revolutionary Year of 1917.

SUGGESTIONS FOR ADDITIONAL READING

This bibliographical note provides only a small and highly selective list of some of the most valuable books on Russia after 1861. For the student who wishes to investigate further, extensive bibliographies listing works in English are presented in many of the specialized studies mentioned below and in recently published textbook histories of Russia, such as those by Anatole Mazour, Nicholas Riasanovsky and Jesse Clarkson. Also, because meritorious scholarly studies on Russian developments after 1861 appear regularly in the pages of the learned journals dedicated to Slavic studies, the inquiring student will find it immensely useful to examine the indices of the *Slavic Review, The Russian Review,* and the *Slavonic and East European Review.*

A number of collective works, often the products of symposia, have been published during the past ten years and are of primary importance. *The Transformation of Russian Society* (Cambridge, Mass., 1960), edited by Cyril E. Black, presents several very authoritative studies on the subject of social change in Russia. *Continuity and Change in Russian and Soviet Thought* (Cambridge, Mass., 1955), edited by Ernest J. Simmons, offers a series of perceptive analyses by distinguished scholars concerned with nineteenth- and twentieth-century intellectual developments. A similar work, *Russian Thought and Politics* (Cambridge, Mass., 1957), edited by Hugh McLean, Martin E. Malia and George Fischer, contains thoughtful and erudite essays by the former students of Michael Karpovich, to whom the book is dedicated. Richard Pipes has edited a smaller collection of articles under the title, *The Russian Intelligentsia* (New York, 1961), in which the first four pieces constitute an admirable effort to define and analyze the character of Russia's pre-revolutionary intelligentsia; and John Sheldon Curtiss is editor of still another collection, *Essays in Russian and Soviet History* (New York, 1963), containing several pieces that contribute much to the understanding of Russia's modernization.

An earlier collective effort of major importance is the multi-volume "Russian Series," produced under the aegis of the Carnegie Endowment for International Peace, as a part of its *Economic and Social History of the War,* and published by the Yale University Press. Among the most valuable works in this series are: B. E. Nolde's *Russia in the Economic War* (1929); T. I. Polner's *Russian Local Government During the War and the Union of Zemstvo's* (1930); and Michael T. Florinsky's summing up, *The End of the Russian Empire* (1930).

Among general studies attempting a broad analysis of the flux of events after 1861 two older works are still very useful. These are the three-volume study by A. Leroy-Beaulieu, *The Empire of the Tsars and the Russians,* translated by Z. A. Ragozin (New York, 1893–1896), and Sir Donald Mackenzie Wallace's *Russia* (New York, 1912). Both authors spent many years in Russia; both were talented observers and sensitive reporters. Michael Karpovich's *Imperial Russia 1801–1917* (New York, 1957) is brief and cogent, but inclined to overstress the hopeful aspects of Russia's progress; *The Decline of Imperial Russia 1855–1914* (New York, 1952), by Hugh Seton-Watson, is a dry but accurate treatment, giving special emphasis to Russia's nationality problems; and Sergei Pushkarev's book, *The Emergence of Modern Russia, 1801–1917* (New York, 1963), is a full and penetrating study. The concise textbook of Donald Treadgold, *Twentieth Century Russia* (New York, 1959), carries its story to 1917 in the first eight chapters, and Volume II of Michael Florinsky's much more detailed *Russia, a History and an Interpretation* (New York, 1953) stresses economic history along with its political narrative. In a much abridged translation, *The Origins of Modern Russia* (New York, 1948), the Polish scholar, Jan Kucharzewski presents his sagacious analysis of Russia's behavior after 1861; and for the student seeking to comprehend the details of Russian life at many levels just before the Revolution of 1905, Henri Troyat's *Daily Life in Russia Under the Last Tsar* (London, 1959) is brief, delightfully interesting and informative.

Of general surveys emphasizing one or another aspect of Russia's development, the philosophical approach is well-handled by both N. O. Lossky, in his *History of Russian Philosophy* (New York, 1951), and V. V. Zenkovsky, in *A History of Russian Philosophy* (New York, 1953). Avrahm Yarmolinsky's *Road to Revolution: A Century of Russian Radicalism* (New York, 1959) is an enthusiastic endorsement of the belief that the revolutionaries were the predominant force for change in Russia; and *Portraits of Russian Personalities: Between Reform and Revolution* (Oxford, 1959), by Richard Hare, provides absorbing but not always deeply-perceptive case studies of Russia's greatest novelists, populists, religious thinkers, and conservative statesmen. In *Lenin and His Rivals: The Struggle for Russia's Future, 1898–1906,* Donald Treadgold presents an objective and sophisticated examination of the intelligentsia's efforts to "set people free" during a crucial period, and while many works have described the shortcomings of the court of Nicholas II, certainly the most convincing and knowledgeable account is that by Bernard Pares, *The Fall of the Russian Monarchy* (New York, 1939).

For the student interested in the ideas and actions of the different groups of radical intelligentsia, there are many valuable materials. Franco Venturi's *Roots of the Revolution* (New York, 1960) is the best account in any language of populist and socialist movements up to 1881. *Red Prelude* (London, 1944), by David Footman, gives a short, dramatic picture of the lives and deaths of the terrorists who assassinated Alexander II, and James H. Billington's *Mikhailovsky and Russian Populism* (Oxford, 1948) presents a brilliant analysis of the populist mastermind of the nineties and his important influence. Arthur P. Mendel discusses and defends the theories of the legal populists in *Dilemmas of Progress in Tsarist Russia: Legal Marxism and Legal Populism* (Cambridge, Mass., 1961); and in an extremely melodramatic book, *Azeff the Spy* (New York, 1934), Boris Nikolaevsky presents a well-documented account of the Social Revolutionary and police agent who organized the assassination of the Minister of the Interior, Pleve, in 1904. The most outstanding analysis of the trials and tribulations of the Social Revolutionaries is the moralizing but richly informative work of Oliver H. Radkey, *The Agrarian Foes of Bolshevism* (New York, 1958).

Samuel H. Baron has written a much-needed and excellent work on "the father of Russian Marxism" in his *Plekhanov* (Stanford, 1963), and Leopold Haimson's *The Russian Marxists and the Origins of Bolshevism* (Cambridge, Mass., 1955) sets forth his judicious and imaginative analysis of the ideas and personalities of Plekhanov, Axelrod, Martov, and Lenin. One of the most vividly-written and interesting books on the rise of the Bolsheviks is *Three Who Made a Revolution* (Boston, 1948), by Bertram Wolfe. In *Social Democracy and the St. Petersburg Labor Movement, 1885–1897* (Cambridge, Mass., 1963), Richard Pipes has made a detailed study of the relations between Russian labor and Social Democracy and of the lessons Lenin drew from this experience; R. Kindersley's work, *The First Russian Revisionists* (London, 1962), is an objective but sympathetic examination of the legal Marxists; and J. L. H. Keep's *The Rise of Social Democracy in Russia* (London, 1963) examines the evolution of the R.S.D.R.P. from its origins through the Revolution of 1905.

Scholarly research on liberalism in Russia is still very thin, although George Fischer's original and provocative theses in *Russian Liberalism* (Cambridge, Mass., 1958) have undoubtedly stimulated others to renewed efforts to understand the liberals' significance. Paul Miliukov's *Russia and Its Crisis* (Chicago, 1905) gives an excellent picture of this liberal leader's view of the Russian situation; and *The Rise of Democracy in Pre-Revolutionary Russia* (New York, 1962), by Jacob Walkin, revives but somewhat ineffectively defends the views of V. A. Maklakov. As with the liberals, so it is with the official-conservatives, where little work of real value has been produced on Russia's high officials. K. P. Pobedonostsev's *Reflections of a Russian Statesman* (London, 1898) is a revelation to the American student. *The Emperor Alexander II* (London, 1962), by E. M. Almedingen, and the small book of W. E. Mosse, *Alexander II and the Modernization of Russia* (London, 1958), are both popularly written and serviceable, but Charles Lowe's work, *Alexander III of Russia* (London, 1895), cries for replacement. Little can be said about the incompetence of Nicholas II and the Empress that they have not said more emphatically in *The Letters of the Tsaritsa to the Tsar, 1914–1916* (London, 1923) and *The Letters of the Tsar to the Tsaritsa, 1914–1917* (New York, 1929).

In economic and institutional research, Western scholars still have much to accomplish. Among the more useful works, James Mavor's *An Economic History of Russia* (2 vols., New York, 1914, 1925) is a bold pioneering synthesis which badly needs updating. Alexander Gershenkron's *Economic Backwardness in Historical Perspective* (Cambridge, Mass., 1962) contains brief, brilliant essays which have greatly influenced contemporary thought about economic development, and Theodore Von Laue's book, *Sergei Witte and the Industrialization of Russia* (New York and London, 1963), is noteworthy for its attention to the industrialization process and to the character and policies of Russia's most gifted Minister of Finance. P. I. Liashchenko's *History of the National Economy of Russia to the 1917 Revolution,* translated from the Russian (New York, 1949) presents the Marxist-Leninist interpretation of an authoritative Soviet scholar. The agricultural sector of Russia's economy has received more careful attention than the industrial, and the best works in this field are: G. T. Robinson, *Rural Russia Under the Old Regime* (2nd ed., New York, 1949); George Pavlovsky, *Agricultural Russia on the Eve of the Revolution* (London, 1930); Launcelot A. Owen, *The Russian Peasant Movement, 1906–1917* (London, 1937); Donald W. Treadgold, *The Great Siberian Migration: Government and Peasant in Resettlement from Emancipation to the First World War* (Princeton, 1957); and A. N. Antsiferov, A. D. Bilimovich, et al, *Russian Agriculture During the War* (New Haven, 1930).

Although much promising research is in progress dealing with the era of the dumas, with Stolypin's reforms and institutional developments after 1905, the principal new studies available have appeared in learned journals. Alfred Levin's excellent work, *The Second Duma: A Study of the Social-Democratic Party and the Russian Constitutional Experiment* (New Haven, 1940), is an early monograph; A. E. Badaev's *The Bolsheviks in the Tsarist Duma* (New York, 1937) is a highly colored defense of Bolshevik tactics by a former Bolshevik delegate; and the immensely instructive book by S. Kucherov, *Courts, Lawyers and Trials Under the Last Three Tsars* (New York, 1953), deals with the 1864 juridical reforms and the lawyers' struggles for the rule of law.

There is a plethora of memoir literature for this period. *Memoirs of a Revolutionist* (New York, 1927; London, 1929), by the populist and Social Revolutionary heroine, Vera Figner, is exciting and informative. The several books of S. M. Kravchinsky (Stepniak) well illustrate the brash naiveté and high dedication of the populists, as does the anarchist Prince Kropotkin's *Memoirs of a Revolutionist* (Boston, 1899). Of similar value are Boris Savinkov's *Memoirs of a Terrorist* (New York, 1931), and *Hidden Springs of the Russian Revolution: The Personal Memoirs of Katerina Breshkovskaia* (Stanford, 1931). While there are innumerable studies on Lenin in English, there is no adequate biographical study; however, Leon Trotsky's insights in his *Lenin* (New York, 1925) are fascinating, and *The Memories of Lenin* (New York, n.d.) by his wife, N. K. Krupskaya, are very rewarding. Louis Fischer's *The Life of Lenin* (New York, 1964) is excellent for Lenin's later years. For official-conservatives the much abridged *Memoirs of Count Witte,* translated and edited by A. Yarmolinsky (New York, 1921) clearly delineates Witte's ideas, his forcefulness and his arrogance. Finally, *Features and Figures of the Past* (Stanford, 1939), by V. I. Gurko, an official at the second level in the Ministry of Internal Affairs, and *Out of My Past* (Stanford, 1935), by V. N. Kokovtsov, who was Minister of Finance from 1904 to 1914 and Chairman of the Council of Ministers from 1911 to 1914, are detailed and enlightening.